Facing Your Fears

Facilitator's Manual

Facing Your Fears

Facilitator's Manual

**Group Therapy for
Managing Anxiety in
Children with High-Functioning
Autism Spectrum Disorders**

by

Judy Reaven, Ph.D.
University of Colorado
Anschutz Medical Campus, School of Medicine
Aurora

Audrey Blakeley-Smith, Ph.D.
University of Colorado
Anschutz Medical Campus, School of Medicine
Aurora

Shana Nichols, Ph.D.
ASPIRE Center for Learning and Development
Melville, New York

and

Susan Hepburn, Ph.D.
University of Colorado
Anschutz Medical Campus, School of Medicine
Aurora

·P A U L·H·
BROOKES
PUBLISHING CO. ®

Baltimore • London • Sydney

Paul H. Brookes Publishing Co.
Post Office Box 10624
Baltimore, Maryland 21285-0624
USA

www.brookespublishing.com

Typeset by Auburn Associates, Inc., Baltimore, Maryland.
Manufactured in the United States of America
by Versa Press, Inc., East Peoria, Illinois.

Cover photo: Philip and Karen Smith/The Image Bank/Getty Images.

The accompanying DVD contains video segments illustrating the intervention discussed in *Facing Your Fears*. The video clips were supplied by the authors, and permission was obtained for all individuals whose faces are shown in footage contained in the DVD.

Supported in part by the National Institutes of Health (NIH) Grant 1R21MH089291-01. However, the content does not necessarily reflect the position of the NIH, and no official endorsement should be inferred.

For information on the *Facing Your Fears* companion products, visit www.brookespublishing.com

Library of Congress Cataloging-in-Publication Data

Reaven, Judy.
  Facing your fears facilitator's manual : group therapy for managing anxiety in children with high-functioning autism spectrum disorders / by Judy Reaven ... [et al.].
     p.   cm.
  Includes bibliographical references and index.
  ISBN-13:   978-1-59857-175-2 (pbk., with bound-in DVD)
  ISBN-10:   1-59857-175-3 (pbk., with bound-in DVD)
  ISBN-13:   978-1-59857-178-3 (set of facilitator manual, parent workbook, child workbook)
  ISBN-10:   1-59857-178-8 (set of facilitator manual, parent workbook, child workbook)
  1. Asperger's syndrome in children.   2. Group psychotherapy for children.   3. Anxiety.   I. Reaven, Judy.   II. Title.
RJ506.A9R43 2011
618.92'858832—dc22   2011005723

British Library Cataloguing in Publication data are available from the British Library.

2015   2014   2013   2012   2011

10   9   8   7   6   5   4   3   2   1

Contents

_____

DVD indicates that a video segment related to a group activity/intervention is available on the accompanying *Facing Your Fears* DVD.

About the Authors

Judy Reaven, Ph.D., Associate Professor, Department of Psychiatry and Pediatrics, JFK Partners, University of Colorado, Anschutz Medical Campus, School of Medicine, 13121 East 17th Avenue, C-234, Aurora, Colorado 80045

Dr. Reaven is a licensed clinical psychologist and has been the director of the Autism and Developmental Disabilities Clinic of JFK Partners since 2001. She has worked in the field of developmental disabilities as a clinician, researcher, and educator since 1985. Clinical and research interests include the co-occurrence of mental health symptoms in children and adolescents with autism spectrum disorders (ASDs), as well as the development of the *Facing Your Fears* program for anxiety symptoms in youth with anxiety and ASDs. She has authored a number of peer-reviewed research articles and has presented nationally and internationally on her clinical research. Dr. Reaven has been Principal Investigator on several research projects funded by private foundations dedicated to autism research (Autism Speaks, Cure Autism Now, The Organization for Autism Research). She is currently the principal investigator on a federally funded project (National Institute of Mental Health), training outpatient clinicians to deliver the *Facing Your Fears* program to youth with anxiety and ASDs.

Audrey Blakeley-Smith, Ph.D., Assistant Professor, Department of Psychiatry and Pediatrics, JFK Partners, University of Colorado, Anschutz Medical Campus, School of Medicine, 13121 East 17th Avenue, C-234, Aurora, Colorado 80045

Dr. Blakeley-Smith is a licensed clinical psychologist and has worked in the field of developmental disabilities since 1996. Current research interests include the assessment and treatment of comorbid mental health issues in children with autism spectrum disorders (ASDs) and the development of peer-mediated interventions in school settings. She is a co-investigator on a National Institute of Mental Health study to train outpatient clinicians in the delivery of the *Facing Your Fears* program. She is also a clinician on a Health Resources and Services Administration–funded study using telemedicine as a medium to treat anxiety in children with ASDs in underserved communities in Colorado. Dr. Blakeley-Smith is currently the principal investigator on a school-based study exploring the use of peer-mediated interventions to reduce rejection and increase inclusion of children with ASDs, funded by The Organization for Autism Research.

Shana Nichols, Ph.D., Founder and Director, ASPIRE Center for Learning and Development, 63 Old East Neck Road, Melville, New York 11747

Dr. Nichols is a licensed clinical psychologist and researcher and has worked in the field of autism spectrum disorders (ASDs) and child development since the mid 1990s. She has received research and service grant support for work in sexuality, puberty, healthy lifestyles, and ASDs, and is the author of several peer-reviewed research articles and invited papers. Dr. Nichols currently specializes in adolescence and growing up, dual diagnosis and mental health, assessment and evaluation, and the experiences of females with ASDs. She is lead author of the book *Girls Growing Up on the Autism Spectrum: What Parents Should Know About the Pre-teen and Teenage Years* (Jessica Kingsley, 2008), with Gina Marie Moravcik and Samara Pulver Tetenbaum. Dr. Nichols has worked as a clinician, researcher, administrator, graduate training supervisor, advisory board member, trainer, and consultant in a wide variety of settings including outpatient clinics, residential programs, schools, and the community.

Susan Hepburn, Ph.D., Associate Professor, Department of Psychiatry and Pediatrics, JFK Partners, University of Colorado, Anschutz Medical Campus, School of Medicine, 13121 East 17th Avenue, C-234, Aurora, Colorado 80045

In addition to her work at the University of Colorado, Anschutz Medical Campus, School of Medicine, Dr. Hepburn is the director of research for JFK Partners, which is the University Center for Excellence in Developmental Disabilities at University of Colorado. Dr. Hepburn is actively involved in intervention and developmental research and has published more than 40 articles in peer-reviewed journals. As a clinical psychologist, she has worked with many children with autism spectrum disorders (ASDs), their families, and school teams, particularly in the development of coping as well as other adaptive behavior skills. Dr. Hepburn is currently the principal investigator of a Health Resources and Services Administration–funded study to explore the use of telemedicine to treat anxiety in children with ASDs in underserved communities in Colorado.

Acknowledgments

This manual could not have been completed without the hard work and support from a number of individuals and organizations. We wish to thank the following research and clinical team members: Stephen Shirk, Lila Kimel, Erin Flanigan, Meena Dasari, Katy Ridge, Joy Browne, Samantha Piper, Michelle Shanahan, Celeste St. John-Larkin, Irene Drmic, Rebecca Schroeder, Terry Hall, Terry Katz, Jennifer Stedron, Amanda Mossman, Jenni Rosenberg, Laura Santerre-Lemmon, Lauren McGrath, Megan Martins, Aime Duncan, Mary Hetrick, Mark Groth, Laura Zapapas, Isabel Smith, Tricia Beattie, April Sullivan, Helen Flanagan, Jamesie Coolican, and Jillian Filliter. Many thanks to Philip Kendall, John Brown, and Karen Frankel for reading through the manuals and providing invaluable feedback. I am grateful for the support of Cure Autism Now, Autism Speaks, the Organization for Autism Research, and the Doug Flutie Foundation, which have partially funded this project. Additional support for this project comes in part from grants awarded to JFK Partners, University of Colorado, Anschutz Medical Campus, School of Medicine from the Administration on Developmental Disabilities, University Center of Excellence in Developmental Disabilities Grant 90DD0632; the Maternal Child Health Bureau, Leadership Education in Neurodevelopmental Disabilities (LEND) Grant T73MC11044; and the Intellectual and Developmental Disabilities Research Center (IDDRC), NICHD funded Translational Neuroscience Nexus P30 HD004024-39. A special thanks to Kathy Culhane-Shelburne for her dedication as our clinical partner and for her countless hours spent working with families and fine-tuning assessment strategies. This manual could not have been completed without the artistic and technical involvement of Kristina Hightshoe or the support of Corry Robinson, director of JFK Partners, as well as the wonderful support and guidance from Rebecca Lazo, Steve Plocher, Leslie Eckard, and all of the other great people at Paul H. Brookes Publishing Co. A final thank-you goes to all of the families who have participated in this project and/or other related projects and therapies. I thank you for your time and your patience. You have taught me so much. A special thanks to Christopher Dosen for technical assistance and direct, non–sugar-coated feedback about the contents of this program.

To my parents Zendra and Mel Ashkanazi,
for their unwavering support,
and for whom the reality of this manual occurred long before I began the work

—J.R.

List of Materials

Session 1

Large Group
- Snacks
- Written schedule, posted on the wall if necessary
- Written list of rules, posted on the wall if necessary
- Playground-style bouncy ball
- Flipcharts with markers

Parent Group
- Pencils and pens

Child Group
- Written schedule
- Sticker cards and stickers
- Paper, pencils, pens, crayons, and markers

Large Group
- Poster board* for list of advice
- Prize basket

Session 2

Large Group
- Snacks
- Written schedule
- Written list of rules

Parent–Child Pairs or Trios
- Pens, pencils, crayons, and markers
- New sticker cards and stickers
- Group rules

Parent Group
- None

Child Group
- Emotions cards and situations
- *Alicia Has a Bad Day* (Jahn-Clough, 1994) or *Alexander and the Terrible, Horrible, No Good, Very Bad Day* (Viorst, 1987), or other similar storybooks

Large Group
- Advice poster
- Prizes for sticker cards

Session 3

Large Group
- Snacks
- Written schedule
- Written list of rules

Parent–Child Pairs or Trios
- None

Parent Group
- None

Child Group
- Pencils, pens, crayons, markers, paper, and scissors
- Sticker cards and stickers
- Set of different-colored Play-Doh or clay
- Bowl for selecting of interests
- Digital camera

Large Group
- Advice poster
- Small prizes for sticker cards

Session 4

Large Group
- Snacks
- Written schedule
- Written list of rules
- Pencils and/or markers
- *Facing Your Fears* video: Relaxation training

Parent–Child Pairs or Trios
- Stress-o-meters (or materials to make them, if time)

---

*Any poster-sized piece of paper could be used throughout the sessions.

Large Group
- Props for Show and Tell
- Advice poster
- Small prizes for sticker cards

Session 5
Large Group
- Snacks
- Written schedule
- Written list of rules
- Pens, pencils, and/or markers

Child Group
- *Parts* (Arnold, 1997)

Parent Group
- None

Large Group
- Small prizes for sticker cards

Session 6
Large Group
- Snacks
- Written schedule
- Written list of rules
- Pens, pencils, and/or markers

Child Group
- *More Parts* (Arnold, 2000)

Parent Group
- None

Large Group
- *Facing Your Fears* video: Dogs

Parent–Child Pairs or Trios
- Pens, pencils, and/or markers
- Small index cards

Large Group
- Small prizes for sticker cards

Session 7
Large Group
- Snacks
- Jar of special treats
- Written schedule
- Written list of rules
- Pens, pencils, and/or markers
- *Facing Your Fears* video: Talking on the Phone

Parent–Child Pairs or Trios
- Pens, pencils, and/or markers
- Stress-o-meters
- Rewards for facing fears and/or participating in role plays

Child Group
- Pens, pencils, and/or markers

Parent Group
- None

Large Group
- Small prizes for sticker cards

Session 8
Large Group
- Snacks
- Jar of special treats
- Written schedule
- Written list of rules
- Pens, pencils, and/or markers

Parent–Child Pairs or Trios
- Completed goal sheets for each of the children
- Stress-o-meters
- Rewards for facing fears and/or participating in role plays

Child Group
- *Facing Your Fears* scripts templates
- Props for filming
- Video camera and film, if needed

Parent Group
- None

Large Group
- Small prizes

Sessions 9–13
Large Group
- Snacks
- Jar of special treats
- Written schedule
- Written list of rules
- Pens, pencils, and/or markers

Parent–Child Pairs or Trios
- Completed goal sheets for each of the children
- Stress-o-meters
- Rewards for facing fears and/or participating in role-plays

Child Group
- Completed template for scripts
- Props for filming
- Video camera and film

Parent Group
- None

Large Group
- Small prizes

Session 14

Large Group

- Jar of special treats

Parent Group

- None

Child Group

- *Parts* or *More Parts*
- Sticker cards and stickers

Large Group

- Videos (*Facing Your Fears*)
- Graduation certificates
- Acting awards

Booster Session

Large Group

- Snacks
- Jar of special treats
- Written schedule
- Written list of rules

Parent—Child Pairs or Trios

- Pens, pencils, and/or markers
- Fresh sticker cards and stickers

Parent Group

- None

Child Group

- *Facing Your Fears* video: Getting Stuck in a Store that Is Closing
- Poster paper, pens, markers
- Large drawings of "stressed" boy and "calm" boy
- Common anxiety-provoking situations written on slips of paper
- Deck of cards with suggestions for helpful thoughts, calming/relaxing activities, and graded exposure

Large Group

- Small prizes

REFERENCES

Arnold, T. (1997). *Parts.* New York: Dial Books for Young Readers.

Arnold, T. (2001). *More parts.* New York: Puffin Books.

Jahn-Clough, L. (1994). *Alicia has a bad day.* Boston: Houghton Mifflin.

Viorst, J. (1972). *Alexander and the terrible, horrible, no good, very bad day.* New York: Aladdin Paperbacks.

Introduction

Facing Your Fears is a program that uses a cognitive-behavioral group therapy approach for the reduction of anxiety symptoms in children with high-functioning autism spectrum disorders (ASD). Anxiety disorders are among the most common psychiatric conditions that present during childhood and often co-occur with other diagnoses, such as disorders of attention, mood, conduct, and development (Compton et al., 2004; Dadds & Barrett, 2001; Kendall, Brady, & Verduin, 2001). Children with high-functioning autism and Asperger syndrome are at high risk for developing symptoms of clinical anxiety (Attwood, 2005; Brereton, Tonge, & Einfeld, 2006; Gillott, Furniss, & Walter, 2001; Lainhart, 1999; Leyfer et al., 2006; Muris, Steerneman, Merckelbach, Holdrinet, & Meesters, 1998). Anxiety can interfere significantly with a child's ability to participate in home, school, and community activities (Russell & Sofronoff, 2005). Children with significant anxiety symptoms are at risk for serious educational problems, later underemployment, substance abuse, and other psychiatric conditions (Velting, Setzer, & Albano, 2004). Furthermore, anxiety can be especially debilitating to individuals with ASD (Greig & MacKay, 2005) by adversely affecting school performance, peer relationships, and family functioning and further exacerbating the core impairments of ASD (Bellini, 2004; Sze & Wood, 2007).

ABOUT THE TREATMENT APPROACH

The literature supporting the effectiveness of cognitive-behavioral therapy (CBT) for reducing anxiety symptoms in typically developing children is vast (Compton et al., 2004; Velting et al., 2004; Walkup et al., 2008). Several published case studies have demonstrated reductions in anxiety symptoms after the implementation of CBT techniques for children and adolescents with ASD (Hare, 1997; Lord, 1995; Reaven & Hepburn, 2003; Sze & Wood, 2007). Additional treatment studies have demonstrated reductions in anxiety symptoms for children with ASD following modified CBT group interventions, which suggests the promising impact of CBT for this population of high-risk individuals (Chalfant, Rapee, & Carroll, 2006; Reaven et al., 2009; Sofronoff, Attwood, & Hinton, 2005; White, Ollendick, Scahill, Oswald, & Albano, 2009; Wood et al., 2009).

Who Can Facilitate the Group Therapy Sessions?

The intervention approach outlined in the *Facing Your Fears* program represents an integration of knowledge from several professional and/or clinical fields—interventions for children with ASD as well as the use of CBT to treat anxiety symptoms in the general pediatric population. Therefore, in this manual, we apply CBT, considered best practice in the general population for reducing anxiety symptoms, to a population that is highly affected by the presence of anxious symptomatology—children and adolescents with ASD. We realize that although many professionals have experience in one field or the other, very few professionals have experience in both arenas. This treatment approach originally was designed to be used by professionals with experience and familiarity in working with CBT in the general population *and/or* by professionals with experience and familiarity in working with children with ASD, with the assumption that experience in one of these main areas is a sufficient prerequisite for the implementation of the manualized intervention. However, in research settings, mental health professionals (e.g., clinical psychologists, clinical psychology graduate students, interns, postdoctoral fellows) have been the main facilitators. Some of these therapists have had extensive experience in working with children with ASD but less experience in conducting CBT interventions. Other facilitators were much more comfortable conducting CBT interventions but had less direct experience in working with children with ASD. Future studies will look at training mental health professionals with CBT experience but limited ASD experience as well as training non–mental health professionals with extensive ASD experience in this approach. Should non–mental health professionals choose to deliver this intervention, it is recommended that they consult with mental health providers because of the psychiatric complexity with which children with high-functioning ASD present.

How *Facing Your Fears* Relates to Other Interventions

Many of the concepts that are outlined in this program are cognitive-behavioral approaches for the reduction of anxiety symptoms in the general pediatric population that have been discussed and written about by various researchers (Barrett, Healy-Farrell, & March, 2004; Chansky, 2004; Cobham, Dadds, & Spence, 1998; Garland & Clark, 1995; Kendall & Hedtke, 2006; March & Mulle, 1998; Mendlowitz et al., 1999; Rapee, Wignall, Hudson, & Schniering, 2000; Schwartz, 1996). Where appropriate, throughout this program, the specific work of other researchers is cited. Many of the activities outlined in this manual are based on long-standing, mainstream cognitive-behavioral concepts that have been modified to meet the cognitive, linguistic, and social needs of children with ASD.

Facing Your Fears, in its own way, keeps the important features of the empirically supported programs that preceded it (e.g., *Coping Cat*; Kendall & Hedtke, 2006) but makes appropriate adaptations for youth with high-functioning autism spectrum disorders. In so doing, *Facing Your Fears* takes on a new arena with a new look. In this program, each group session is tailored to address the specific needs of children with ASD who also present with anxiety-related symptoms. In addition, parent participation is an integral component to this treatment approach. Throughout the program, the parents' roles and expectations are interwoven throughout each group session. We feel that the children's success in reducing their anxiety symptoms may be heavily dependent on parental involvement, particularly for younger children.

RUNNING THE PROGRAM

The *Facing Your Fears* program is composed of three books and a DVD. The three books include a workbook for parents; a workbook for children; and this facilitator's manual for therapists that includes goals, objectives, and activities for each group session. The 14-week group therapy treatment includes the following core components of CBT—introduction and psychoeducation of anxiety symptoms, awareness of automatic negative thoughts and development of coping statements, somatic management of physical symptoms of anxiety, use of graded exposure to face fears, and relapse prevention. Because children with ASD present with social impairments that may underlie and/or potentially exacerbate anxiety symptoms, development of social skills that may directly relate to specific fears and/or worries are included in the treatment. The question of child readiness and preparedness always needs to be asked before an exposure step: Does the child possess the skills necessary for the exposure step to be successful? If not, how can these skills specifically be taught to the child to ensure his or her successful completion of the hierarchy step? There is much focus on practicing and applying these skills and other "tools" taught in group sessions across settings, including the use of these tools during in vivo role plays, real situations that naturally occur in the child's environment, and exposure sessions in group and/or at home.

Who Should Participate?

This program is specifically designed for work with children with high-functioning ASD, though there is no specific mention of ASD throughout the intervention. This program was intended for children with ASD who have primarily average intellectual ability (e.g., approximate verbal IQ score of 80 or higher) and who are able to read at the second-grade level; therefore, the extent to which it would be effective for children with marked cognitive impairments is unclear. Furthermore, the anxiety diagnoses targeted by this intervention include social phobia, generalized anxiety disorder, separation anxiety disorder, and specific phobia (see research section below). These diagnoses should be considered the child's primary comorbid diagnosis. In other words, if a child's symptoms of depression or obsessive compulsive disorder appear to be more impairing than the child's social phobia, generalized anxiety disorder, separation anxiety disorder, or specific phobia, then this intervention would not be considered appropriate. Given the psychiatric complexity of children with ASD, a comprehensive assessment is recommended to sort through these issues. Although the primary purpose of this program is to enhance the accessibility of CBT interventions for children with ASD, given the linguistic and cognitive challenges of children with other developmental disabilities or learning difficulties, the program also may enhance the accessibility of CBT interventions for children with other special learning needs.

How to Facilitate the Groups

The *Facing Your Fears Facilitator's Manual: Group Therapy for Managing Anxiety in Children with High-Functioning Autism Spectrum Disorders* outlines each group session with specific instructions for how to conduct each session. Between four and five families (including at least one parent and the child) are asked to attend weekly, 1 1/2-hour group sessions for 14 consecutive weeks. The sessions include large-group time (parents and children together), parents alone and children alone (to occur simultaneously), and work in parent–child pairs or trios. To most effectively deliver the treatment package, we recommend a minimum of three facilitators—one facilitator for the parent's group and two for the children's group. Prior group treatment experience is highly recommended for each facilitator. Each session outline in the facilitator's manual includes the primary purpose of the session, specific goals and/or objectives for the session, and activities for working within each of the modalities—parents alone, children alone, parent–child pairs or trios, and the large group.

Parent Groups

We view parents as critical to children's success in treatment. The parent component of the *Facing Your Fears* program includes the following: 1) psychoeducation of anxiety disorders and introduction to the basic principles of CBT, 2) identification of the child's specific anxiety symptoms, 3) identification of target behaviors in preparation for graded-exposure assignments, 4) discussion of parental anxiety and parenting styles, and 5) discussion of the social and communicative challenges inherent in ASD and how these challenges may lead to a protective parenting style (Reaven & Hepburn, 2006). The concepts of *adaptive protection* and *excessive protection* are introduced to the parents. *Adaptive protection,* on the one hand, is defined as a useful parental response that occurs when children present with marked areas of developmental, physical, or emotional challenge. Because children with extensive challenges may experience many realistic fears in their everyday lives, their parents and other caregivers must titrate their children's exposure to challenging environmental events to create multiple success experiences for them over time. *Excessive protection,* on the other hand, may limit a child's exposure to anxiety-provoking situations through avoidant behavior even when the child possesses the necessary skills for success, thus limiting the opportunity to generate and practice effective coping strategies for handling anxiety-provoking situations. We believe that at the heart of a child's successful reduction of anxiety symptoms is his or her parents' creation and appropriate implementation of the child's exposure hierarchy; therefore, much of the time spent in final sessions of the group is focused on ensuring parental understanding of these core concepts. Finally, discussions about how to share coping skills and the creation of exposure hierarchies with other family members and/or other professionals occur throughout the sessions so that the gains made in group can be generalized to other settings.

Child Groups

Group sessions for the children are interactive and activity-based. Consistent with other CBT programs (Kendall & Hedtke, 2006; March & Mulle, 1998), there are two primary facets of the *Facing Your Fears* intervention: 1) an introduction to anxiety symptoms with an emphasis on the individual expression of anxiety symptoms in each participant as well as an introduction to common CBT strategies and 2) a focus on the implementation and generalization of specific tools and strategies to treat the anxiety symptoms. Children and parents participate in a series of activities designed to help identify each child's worries and anxiety-induced behaviors, or physical signs and symptoms of anxiety. The connection between the body's reaction and cognitive interpretation of the physiological responses is emphasized. In this step, children and parents are encouraged to "externalize" anxiety symptoms (March & Mulle, 1998; White & Epston, 1990), creating "worry bugs" and "helper bugs" that represent worry and fighting worry, respectively. In this way, the child and his or her parents and therapists are all on a team to fight anxiety together. Tools such as deep breathing, expansion of participation in calming activities on a daily basis, recognition of automatic negative thoughts ("active minds"; Garland & Clark, 1995), and development of positive coping statements ("helpful thoughts") are all taught to the children to help them "fight" anxiety. The children and their parents use a *stress-o-meter* to measure anxiety and heighten awareness of calm and relaxed states versus periods of high stress or anxiety. Then, parent–child pairs or trios create a hierarchy of anxiety-provoking situations, targeting specific fears or worries (both at home and/or school and in group) that are interfering with day-to-day functioning. A primary focus of the intervention is to encourage and reward the children for engaging in graded-exposure tasks (facing fears a little at a time) from their stimulus hierarchies of anxiety-provoking situations. Because social impairments likely underlie some of the specific anxiety symptoms, the treatment also includes segments on social skills building. In efforts to enhance generalization of skills across settings, the participants also write, direct, and star in a series of short *Facing Your Fears* videos depicting children facing their fears in a variety of contexts (Kendall & Hedtke, 2006). The DVD included with the facilitator's manual features several examples of *Facing Your Fears* videos. These films provide an opportunity for participants to observe their peers modeling positive coping strategies and can serve as a form of social learning and cognitive rehearsal.

Booster Session

A booster session is included at the end of the facilitator's manual and workbooks. Facilitators may schedule booster sessions anywhere from 4 to 6 weeks posttreatment. Many traditional CBT protocols include booster sessions, and it has been our experience as well that families often request a refresher session for both themselves and their children to review the main content of the group. The booster session primarily provides the opportunity to review the core principles of the group (i.e., identifying the children's favorite "tools" for handling anxiety—calming and/or relaxing activities, "helpful thoughts," and graded exposure) and discuss how these familiar strategies can be used to tackle the onset of additional symptoms.

TIPS FOR SUCCESS

As with most clinical interventions, one key to success is to engage and establish rapport with all of the participants throughout the treatment process. This is particularly important for children with ASD. Some of the children may never have been members of a structured group before and may experience much discomfort attending a group with other children they do not know. Because of this, many of the initial group activities are designed to support the children to become comfortable in the group session and work to establish relationships with the other group members as well as the facilitators. Every effort has been made to ensure that the pace of each session meets the needs of the children; the core content is presented to the children in enjoyable but small, manageable chunks, alternating content with "down time." Although this is a manualized intervention, the facilitators are encouraged to work their way through the treatment in a flexible manner while striving to maintain the integrity of the content of the materials (Kendall & Beidas, 2007). Facilitators are encouraged to read through the manual carefully before beginning the treatment process to become familiar with the concepts prior to working with the children and their families. Opportunities to practice and reinforce social skills are abundant when working with children in a group context. We have attempted to highlight a few such opportunities along with potential strategies to reinforce these skills in the beginning of each session in the sections titled Social Skills and Suggestions for Supporting Social Skills, respectively. Sentences in *italic type* are designed to be suggestions for verbatim explanations or directions facilitators can give during group activities. Also, watch for the Helpful Hint sidebars throughout the manual for extra pointers on working with the children and their parents.

We want to increase treatment adherence (i.e., following through with homework) throughout this intervention. Completion of homework is equally, if not more, important than the work that takes place during the group. The facilitators should do the following when making assignments: 1) regularly assess the difficulty of the homework recommendations (e.g., Do the parents think it is too hard to do?), 2) make sure parents and children understand *why* they are doing what they are doing, 3) help the parents and children understand how little time the homework tasks actually will take, 4) model behaviors and interactions with the children (for parents) when possible (e.g., during exposure tasks), and 5) encourage rewards for homework compliance.

Suggestions for Children Who Are Not Group-Ready

It has been our experience that group treatment may not be appropriate at the current time for some children with ASD and anxiety. These children may have extreme difficulty separating from their parents, may display aggressive or highly disruptive behaviors, or may have other psychiatric symptoms that may require more intensive interventions (e.g., major depression, psychosis). For research purposes, we have outlined specific behavioral criteria to help determine when a child may be able to participate in group treatment. For example, to be eligible or appropriate for group work, a child must demonstrate the ability to be in a room adjacent to the parent for a minimum of 30 minutes as observed during the assessment sessions. We recommend a trial period of three treatment sessions for facilitators to assess children for group readiness. The child's inability to separate from a parent, the presence of aggressive outbursts, or chronic resistance to treatment may be potential indicators of a lack of group readiness. If within three consecutive sessions (at any point in the treatment) the child is not able to participate without marked distress that cannot be abated by the facilitators, the lead facilitator may make the decision to stop the child's participation in the group and move the family into an individual treatment modality. Although these guidelines were established for conducting research, these same guidelines also may be helpful when conducting clinical groups.

Some children may begin in individual therapy with a goal of working toward being able to participate in a group therapy experience. Moving a child from an individual treatment modality to group treatment can be a gradual and slow process. In clinical settings, it has been most helpful to show the children and their families episodes of the *Facing Your Fears* videos. Again, these are available on the accompanying DVD. Viewing these videos has been remarkably helpful in demonstrating to potential group members what the groups are like. Establishing rapport and helping a child and his or her family feel comfortable in the therapeutic environment may take some time. Gradually increasing periods of time during the sessions when anxiety-related topics are discussed with the remainder of the session devoted to rapport building may work well for some children. It has also been helpful for therapists to set extremely small goals for the children when facing fears in order to achieve success. Lots of repetition and practice have been helpful as well. The extent to which children with ASD and anxiety respond differentially to group and individual treatment is an empirical question, as are the specific characteristics of children and families who respond positively to treatment. As more research studies are completed in this area, we will be in a better position to make treatment recommendations for children who present with this complex set of symptoms.

RESEARCH ON THE *FACING YOUR FEARS* INTERVENTION PROGRAM

One of the most rewarding aspects of clinical work with children with ASD and their families is the potential for positive change. Sometimes the goals of treatment are quite clear-cut—we may endeavor to help a child to learn to communicate, to share toys with another child, or to tolerate a tedious trip to the grocery store. These are relatively simple outcomes to measure because one can define behavioral targets and observe and record their absence or presence. Other times, the outcomes we are focused on in treatment are more difficult to measure and reflect an interpersonal process, often between a parent and a child or a teacher and a student. Self-regulation, or the ability to cope with strong feelings and competing impulses, is an example of one of these more complex treatment outcomes.

Measuring progress in self-regulation involves tapping both within-child and within-system (e.g., family) variables. It encompasses a dynamic, constantly changing set of factors embedded within a dynamic, constantly changing background of developmental challenges. For example, appropriate coping skills for a 4-year-old are quite distinct from those expected from a 10-year-old. For children with ASD, whose development is often splintered and uneven, it can be very difficult to determine appropriate expectations for coping—as many parents ask "Should we push him to handle it or prevent him from having to deal with it?"

As researchers, we ask ourselves parallel questions with regard to outcomes: Is it a success if a parent anticipates an overwhelming situation and structures the experience so that the child doesn't experience too much distress? Or, is a more beneficial outcome defined by coaching the child to face his fears, even if he doesn't cope very well in that moment, knowing that in the long term the child is building a learning history that is not characterized by avoidance or dependence on another person?

These are difficult questions to answer, both from a clinical perspective and with regard to intervention research. As we have tried to study the impact of our intervention over the past several years, we have become increasingly aware of the limitations inherent to studying such complex processes in such a diverse group of families. It is our intention to offer this intervention manual for use by knowledgeable clinicians who can bring the difficult to define "art" to the emerging science within which we are presently engaged. In the next few paragraphs, we will summarize what our research on this intervention approach—collectively the work of the authors, Judy Reaven, Audrey Blakeley-Smith, Shana Nichols, and Susan Hepburn—has revealed, with the caveat that the work is most certainly ongoing.

Results from an Initial Case Study

In 2003, we completed a case study focused on our efforts to implement a modified CBT protocol with a 7-year-old girl with Asperger syndrome and obsessive-compulsive disorder (Reaven & Hepburn, 2003). This study was based on our clinical experiences conducting psychotherapy with individuals with ASD who had different levels of functioning and differing amounts of parent involvement. We observed a decrease in symptom severity and interference after approximately 3 months of treatment, accompanied by a brightening in the child's affect and an increase in her sense of self-efficacy to manage future triggers. Although some of the girl's obsessions and compulsions decreased markedly with treatment, new ones seemed to emerge; and the child and parents reported that having a framework, or an approach that they could employ with new challenges, gave them a sense of hope that the child's anxiety disorder was manageable even if it was not eliminated. In discussions of the 7-year-old girl's progress in therapy, we realized that there were several modifications to traditional CBT protocols that we had integrated into her treatment, and we began to wonder if these intervention elements could be operationalized and methodically delivered to other children.

Clinical and Research Development

Over the next few years, Judy Reaven led the effort to manualize the intervention and, along with Audrey Blakeley-Smith and Shana Nichols, psychology postdoctoral fellows, interns and advanced graduate students contributed significantly to its structure and content. Philip Kendall and Stephen Shirk provided expert consultation that greatly affected the development of this program of research. The current version represents the seventh major revision and reflects the addition of two more sessions, which we have found useful for providing children with increased opportunities to practice exposure. Simultaneously, Susan Hepburn focused on developing the research protocol, defining recruitment and qualification criteria, piloting measures of anxiety symptoms, and attempting to capture the impact of those symptoms on the child and the family. Particular care was taken to develop a protocol that was consistent with ethical principles of practice in psychology. Audrey Blakeley-Smith broadened the assessment battery to include more "real-life" outcomes and has been instrumental in developing a version of the program specifically for adolescents. The research team also developed measures of the intervention process such as treatment fidelity checklists (i.e., what should the therapists be doing in each session), measures of family adherence to the protocol (i.e., what strategies families actually are using outside of group sessions), and measures of child and parent satisfaction with the intervention.

Participant Recruitment and Enrollment

Since 2004, 308 families have contacted the Autism and Anxiety Research Team (ART) at the University of Colorado, Anschutz Medical Campus, to express interest in the treatment studies. Approximately 248 families met screening eligibility and 152 families consented to the qualifying battery. All 152 families completed the qualifying evaluation for the study and 21 children were not eligible; therefore, 131 families from the Denver area were invited to participate in the intervention studies. Families were invited to participate if their child had a diagnosis of generalized anxiety disorder, specific phobia, social phobia, and/or separation anxiety disorder, and if this diagnosis was considered a primary presenting problem (i.e., the child did not have a comorbid diagnosis such as depression that was considered to be causing more significant interference than the anxiety diagnosis).

Youth with ASD entered the program into a School-Age cohort (i.e., ages 7–13 years; $n = 92$; mean age = 10 1/2 years; $SD = 22$ months) or an Adolescent cohort (i.e., 13–19 years; $n = 39$; mean age = 16 years; $SD = 11$ months). Specific ASD diagnoses were autism: $n = 57, 54.3\%$; pervasive developmental disorder–not otherwise specified: $n = 6, 5.7\%$; or Asperger syndrome: $n = 42; 40\%$. Approximately 8% of the sample was Hispanic/Latino; 86% were white, 8% were African American; 5% were Asian/Pacific Islander, and 1% were Native American. Parents were predominantly married and living together (74.3%). Fourteen families had experienced divorce (13.3%), and seven of these parents remarried (6.7%). Almost 10% of the sample was never married, and 3% were widowed. The sample was well educated, with 8.6% of mothers completing high school only, 30.5% completing some college, 40% graduating from college, and 20.9% completing college and postgraduate work. Most families lived within 25 miles of Denver; however, 4 families from rural Colorado commuted more than 60 miles each way to the intervention sessions.

Psychiatric Complexity of Participants

The Anxiety Disorders Interview Schedule for Children–Parent Version (ADIS–P; Silverman & Albano, 1996; $n = 63$) was used to determine which *Diagnostic and Statistical Manual of Mental Disorders* (DSM-IV-TR; American Psychiatric Association, 2000) diagnoses were met for each youth and which were of primary clinical concern. Reliability of diagnostic classifications was computed by two psychologists for 22 interviews; interrater reliability ranged from 76% to 100%, with a mean reliability of 94%. Of 26 possible psychiatric diagnoses probed, the youth with ASD in this sample presented with a range of between 1 and 10 and a median of 5 psychiatric disorders. Rates of diagnoses for our four primary diagnoses in this sample were as follows: generalized anxiety disorder: 93.3%, specific phobia: 83.8%, social phobia: 43.8%, and separation anxiety disorder: 40%.

Process Measures

Family participation and clinician adherence were measured.

Family Participation

The completion rate for the intervention study was 84.7%. Attrition prior to treatment was 8.2%, and attrition during active treatment was approximately 7.1%. Pre- and posttreatment data were collected on 86 youth with ASD and their families. Follow-up data on anxiety symptoms were obtained at 3 months posttreatment for 43 families and at 6–12 months posttreatment for 40 families. In total, the team conducted 22 intervention groups, serving 89 children and their families. Attendance was taken at every group, and 74 of 89 participating families (83%) did not miss any of the twelve treatment sessions; 9 families (10%) missed one session; and 6 families (6.7%) missed two to three sessions (and participated in individual makeup sessions with their lead therapist). None of the families missed more than three sessions, which was the minimal requirement to continue in group.

Clinician Adherence

Clinician adherence to the manualized protocol was assessed using a fidelity rating system developed by the ART. Overall, 96% of observed treatment sessions between 2006 and 2008 met criteria for fidelity. Interobserver agreement on the fidelity checklist ranged from .82–1.00, with an average overall percent agreement of 96%. When a clinician did not demonstrate adequate adherence to the protocol, additional training was employed and fidelity was reassessed. Only 2 of 14 clinicians required additional training. Family satisfaction with the intervention was assessed using an anonymous checklist completed at the end of treatment by the parent and the youth with ASD. Ninety-six percent of parents and eighty-two percent of youth reported feeling "satisfied" or "very satisfied" with the intervention.

The first efficacy study conducted by the ART Team was a small pilot study examining the efficacy of *Facing Your Fears* as compared with a wait-list comparison group who continued to receive treatment as usual in the community. This study, conducted by Reaven and colleagues (2009), included 33 school-age children and their parents. Overall, *Facing Your Fears* demonstrated potential efficacy in decreasing parental report of anxiety severity and interference. Limitations of this study included small sample size, lack of randomization, and lack of an independent evaluator who could be blinded to the child's treatment condition.

The second study, a randomized controlled trial using independent clinical evaluators, was designed to address some of the limitations of the first study (Reaven, Blakeley-Smith, Culhane-Shelburne & Hepburn, in preparation). This study included randomized assignment to either *Facing Your Fears* (FYF) or to treatment as usual (TAU). Fifty-two children between the ages of 7 and 14 years, with estimated full-scale IQ scores ranging from 63 to 140, participated in this study. This sample was predominantly male and Caucasian, with relatively well-educated parent participants, and is not, therefore, a particularly culturally diverse sample.

An independent clinical evaluator (ICE) interviewed parents before and after the intervention phase using the ADIS–P (Silverman & Albano, 1996). In addition, parents completed the Screen for Child Anxiety-Related Emotional Disorders (SCARED; Birmaher et al., 1999). The ICE was not aware of the family's treatment condition assignment and administered the interview in a standardized manner. The primary outcome measures for this study included 1) diagnostic status of target anxiety disorders (e.g., generalized, separation, social, and specific phobia); 2) the ICE's Clinical Global Impression Scale of Severity (CGIS–S; Guy & Bonato, 1976) before and after treatment based on results of the ADIS-P and the SCARED; and 3) the ICE's Clinical Global Impressions Scale of Improvement (CGIS–I; Guy & Bonato, 1976) based on a 7-point scale, with lower numbers indicating more significant improvement.

Results

Results from the second study were very promising, with positive changes in diagnostic status, anxiety symptom severity, and anxiety symptom improvement.

Diagnostic Status Of the participants in the FYF condition, 66.6% demonstrated a positive change in diagnostic status for one or more targeted anxiety disorders, as compared with 20% of participants in the TAU condition. See Figure 1.1 for changes in number of diagnoses per participant. In the FYF group, the 18 participants started with 54 anxiety disorder diagnoses out of a possible 72 (only counting separation anxiety, social phobia, specific phobia, and generalized anxiety disorder). In the TAU group, the 15 participants started with 44 anxiety disorder diagnoses out of a possible 60; therefore, both groups initially presented with approximately 73%–75% of possible diagnoses. By the end of the 5-month treatment period, the FYF group lost 19 diagnoses (reduction of 35.19%) and the TAU group lost 5 diagnoses (reduction of 11.36%). Six out of eight children (75%) in the FYF group who initially met criteria for separation anxiety no longer met criteria for the diagnosis after treatment. Similarly, 5 out of 16 children (31%) with social phobia lost the diagnosis after FYF, 2 out of 15 children (13.3%) lost a specific phobia diagnosis, and 6 out of 16 children (37.5%) no longer met criteria for a generalized anxiety disorder. By comparison, children in the TAU condition were observed to make the following changes in diagnostic status over time: 1 out of 5 (20%) no longer met criteria for a separation anxiety disorder, 1 out of 11 (9%) lost social phobia, none of the 10 children with specific phobia

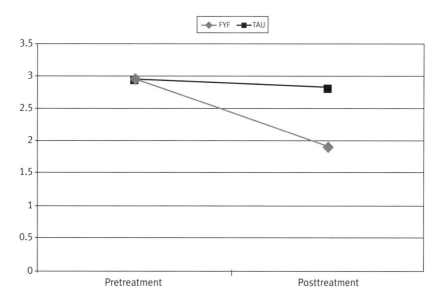

Figure 1.1. Change in mean number of anxiety diagnoses per child by treatment condition (n = 33). Anxiety diagnoses = Separation anxiety, Social phobia, Specific phobia, Generalized Anxiety, maximum possible is 4. (Key: FYF = *Facing Your Fears*; TAU = Treatment as usual.)

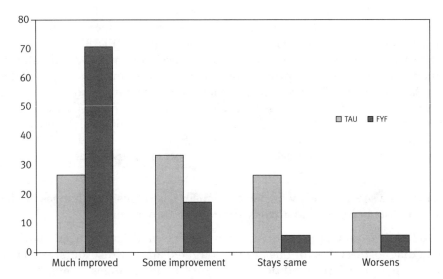

Figure 1.2. Independent clinical evaluator's ratings of improvement across treatment periods. (*Key:* FYF = Facing Your Fears; TAU = Treatment As Usual.)

changed diagnosis over the treatment period, and 2 out of 15 children (13.3%) no longer met criteria for generalized anxiety disorder by the end of the trial. Further study will examine whether this pattern of results holds up over time, suggesting that the FYF intervention may positively affect separation anxiety, generalized anxiety disorder, and social phobia but have less of an impact on specific phobias.

Independent Clinical Evaluator's Clinical Global Impression Scale of Severity   Using a repeated measures analysis of variance technique, specifically a generalized estimating equations (GEE) method with a multinomial distribution, we detected a significant decrease in anxiety symptom severity from pre- to posttreatment for children in the FYF intervention (p = .01). There were no significant differences in anxiety symptom severity for the TAU condition.

Independent Clinical Evaluator's Clinical Global Impression Scale of Improvement   Change in clinician's rating of improvements in anxiety symptoms from pre- to posttreatment was examined using a generalized lineal model with a multinomial distribution (see Figure 1.2). There were significant differences in clinician ratings of improvement as a function of treatment condition (p = .012). In the FYF condition, 70.6% of children were reported to be much improved, 17.6% were reported to improve moderately, 5.9% were reported to stay the same, and 5.9% were reported to worsen in anxiety symptom expression over time. In the TAU condition, 26.7% of children were found by the ICE to be much improved over time, 33.3% were moderately improved, 26.9% stayed the same, and 13.3% were reported to worsen in anxiety symptom expression over time. There was a large effect size for change in improvement: .84 (Cohen's D).

CONCLUSION

In summary, we are excited by the findings of our research. Significant improvements in anxiety symptoms, along with significant changes in diagnostic status and severity of anxiety symptoms have been found post-treatment. Parent and child attendance has been excellent, and satisfaction questionnaires completed posttreatment indicate that families and children enjoy the activities in the *Facing Your Fears* program. Thus, our data indicate that the *Facing Your Fears* program is a feasible group intervention for the treatment of anxiety symptoms in children with high-functioning autism spectrum disorders. Although more research is needed to continue to explore the effectiveness of the *Facing Your Fears* program, we are excited to publish this initial version of the program and hope that clinicians, children, and families will benefit from the strategies outlined in the manual and workbooks.

Future Directions In the general pediatric population, cognitive-behavioral interventions are considered "evidence-based treatment" as defined by the American Psychological Association. However, CBT for children with autism spectrum disorders is considered an "emerging treatment" as defined by the National Standards Report (National Autism Center, 2009). An emerging treatment is when "one or more studies suggest the intervention may produce favorable outcomes"; however, additional high-quality studies that consistently show these treatments to be effective for individuals with ASD are needed (National Autism Center, 2009, pp. 57–69). More rigorous studies, with larger samples and conducted by groups outside of our own clinic, are necessary to firmly establish this treatment program as an empirically based intervention. More work also is needed to identify who responds best to this approach, how to effectively train clinicians to implement the model to fidelity, and whether alternative methods of delivery (such as through a telehealth application or a self-study module) would be effective. Newly funded studies in our research lab are pursuing these questions and will likely add to our knowledge while introducing new challenges along the way. As with any form of clinical work with families of children with ASD, deeper understanding comes from experience working with many different families, each of whom presents with a unique set of strengths and challenges. We anticipate that we will continue to learn from each family that engages in this treatment and from professionals who attempt to implement it in various settings. We hope that subsequent versions of this program will evolve as our understanding of how to promote coping in children with ASD deepens.

Welcome to Group

Words We Use for Worry

Session 1 is intended for the children and their parents to begin to get to know each other and learn about the purpose, goals, and direction of the group. During this session, you should review the rules for the group and provide and discuss a written schedule outlining activities for the day. It will also be helpful during this session to begin to establish a common or shared vocabulary for describing anxious symptoms. Parents will exchange contact information and will generate a list of rewards that can be used to assist with motivating their child to participate in activities throughout the intervention.

SESSION STRUCTURE

- Large group, children and parents together
- Parent group and child group breakout sessions (occur simultaneously)
- Large group, children and parents together, for closing

SAMPLE SCHEDULE—WELCOME TO GROUP: WORDS WE USE FOR WORRY[1]

- **Large Group** (45–50 minutes)
  - Snack
  - Discussion about group
  - Getting-to-know-you game

- **Parent Group** (25–30 minutes)

- **Child Group** (25–30 minutes)
  - Visual schedule
  - Rules for group
  - Sticker program
  - Drawings for workbook covers
  - Emotion words

- **Large Group** (10 minutes)
  - Advice for friends
  - Prizes

SOCIAL SKILLS

- Greeting others; learning names of peers, parents, and facilitators

---

[1]A sample schedule will be provided at the beginning of each session so that facilitators can write the schedule on a large white board or poster paper to visually display the plan for the day. The schedule is written primarily for the children's benefit; therefore, the content of the parent group will not be outlined here. The time estimates are for facilitator use only—some activities may take longer or shorter than predicted.

- Talking in front of a group; sharing personal likes and dislikes
- Listening to others and learning about others' likes and dislikes
- Asking questions and making comments
- Increasing emotion vocabulary

Suggestions for Supporting Social Skills

- Encourage effort and any approximation toward participation, but do not force.
- Provide verbal prompts. (Parents and facilitators can provide these.)
- Model social skills.
- Use rewards for participation.
- Initially model providing brief bits of factual information (e.g., "I like pizza," "My favorite movie is *Cars*") during the getting-to-know-you activity so that the children view sharing with the group as doable.

▌▌▌▌▌▌ Large Group (Children and Parents Together)

Materials and/or Worksheets

- Snacks
- Written schedule
- Written list of rules, posted on the wall if necessary
- Playground-style bouncy ball
- Flipcharts with markers

Goals

1. The children and parents will learn the names of all of the group members and facilitators.
2. The parents and children will learn the two main rules of group: listening to others (e.g., no interrupting) and helping friends when they are feeling worried or anxious (e.g., ignoring silly behavior, making positive or encouraging comments to each other). Offer a few examples.
3. The children and parents will discuss why they are attending group and begin to talk about what they hope to gain from group.
4. The children and parents will learn a few interesting facts about the other participants, including favorite foods, television shows, things to do for fun, and so forth.
5. The children will follow the visual schedule of the group's daily activities and check off each activity once it has been completed.
6. The children and parents will begin to learn a common or shared vocabulary for talking about anxiety or worry.

Helpful Hint   Be aware that some children may be extremely apprehensive and nervous about entering the room. If possible, find out ahead of time from the parents if this may be a problem for their children so that you can plan accordingly. If some children refuse to enter the large group, do not push them to participate at this point; instead, visually show them the schedule for the group and praise and/or reward any participation. Initially, it is important to help the children know what to expect during the activities. You can always decrease

(continued)

the number of people around the child to help him or her warm up slowly as he or she begins to participate in group activities. Alternatively, you may allow parents to speak for their children in the larger group setting because simply attending a large group may be anxiety-provoking for some children. Shortening large-group time also may be an option, particularly if it is clear that the large-group time is too overwhelming for several children. It may be helpful to ask family members in the beginning of Session 1 what kinds of things are rewarding for their children and then to use these rewards liberally throughout the program but particularly in the initial phase of intervention. After the completion of the large-group activity, children and parents will be asked to divide into separate groups. Some children may find it difficult to separate from their parents. Parents can accompany their children to the smaller group, staying with them initially but then gradually weaning themselves away from their children to join the parent group. Rewards may be used to enhance the children's motivation to handle the separation appropriately. Written information about the group content is always available for parents if they miss portions of the parent group.

Activities

1. *Snack:* Provide a variety of drinks and snack foods for parents and children when they arrive for group.
2. *Discussion:* Ask the children and parents why they are in group and what they have been told and/or understand about the group. There is no need to go into great detail about anxiety or worry at this point; it is important simply to offer an initial description for the purpose of the group. It will also be important to make a few logistical points, for example, noting that the structure of the sessions will vary: Sometimes the group will meet as a large group (children and parents together), sometimes parents and children will meet separately, and sometimes the children and their parents will work in pairs or trios.

   It will be important to begin a discussion about the rules for group (e.g., no interrupting, ignore silly behavior, make positive comments). Group rules can be reiterated again during the child group.

   The section below is intended as a suggestion for a verbatim explanation of the purpose of group. Look for other italicized-type scripts throughout the manual.

   Everyone has times when they get scared or worried. Sometimes worry and fear get so big that it is hard to manage and can interfere with our ability to have fun, go to school, or get work done. In this group, we help you (parents and children) identify the situations or things that make you worried or anxious and learn ways to cope with the worry so that it does not get in the way of your having fun, making friends, or participating in school.

3. *Getting-to-know-you activity:* Facilitators, parents, and children form a large circle. A large, playground-style bouncy ball is bounced or passed from one person in the group to another. One of the facilitators begins by identifying a category of favorites (e.g., food, television show, movie, toy, subject in school, place to visit, thing to do for fun, famous person, book, state, sport, game) and then passes the ball to another person in the circle. When a person has the ball, he or she has to give a response in the category identified, call out the name of the person to whom he or she is going to pass the ball, then pass the ball to that group member. This continues until everyone has a chance to give an answer. If a child forgets the name of a group member, the facilitator can coach the child to ask for the peer's name before he or she throws the ball to him or her.

   After one category has been completed, go on to another category. Ask the children and/or parents to generate categories, too. One facilitator should keep notes of all of the children's "favorites," write them on flipcharts under each child's name, and then informally quiz the children at the end of this activity to see what they remember about each other's favorites. For example, "Whose favorite food is pizza?"

Helpful Hint A primary purpose of the getting-to-know-you activity is to help children and parents see that they are unique individuals with a variety of interests and favorite activities that are unrelated to their anxiety symptoms. You are laying the foundation for helping the children and parents create productive ways of spending their time rather than wasting their time on worry and anxiety. We have found that it is effective for the facilitators to emphasize that *everyone* has periods of worry and anxiety, including the parents and facilitators themselves. Throughout the group intervention, it can be helpful for the facilitators to encourage parents to provide examples of their own worry and anxiety and how they have handled the symptoms. In addition, facilitators are similarly encouraged to provide their own personal examples of worry and anxiety that may illustrate core concepts throughout the treatment. Of course, care should be taken on the part of the facilitators to find the right balance with regard to how much personal information they share.

END—GROUP DIVIDES INTO PARENT GROUP AND CHILD GROUP

Parent Group

Materials and/or Worksheets

- Contact Information worksheet (to be compiled into a roster; this worksheet also appears in the Parent Workbook.)
- Brainstorming Goals! worksheet
- Reinforcer Assessment worksheet
- Pencils and pens

Goals

1. The participants will learn more about the purpose, direction, rules, and limitations of the group as well as discuss a plan for ongoing communication with the group facilitators and each other.
2. The participants will learn about the use of positive reinforcement during the course of the treatment.
3. The participants will complete three parent worksheets: Contact Information, Brainstorming Goals, and Reinforcer Assessment

Activities

1. *Discussion:* Logistics and/or parameters of the group

- Discuss the importance of confidentiality among participants; for example, personal information shared in the group should not be shared with individuals outside of the group.
- Facilitators will set up the parameters for communication between the parents and group leaders. You can promote discussion among members by disseminating telephone numbers and e-mail information (assuming you have permission) and indicating that they may want to use each other as a sounding board for concerns. Facilitators can discuss their availability for between-session contacts, although it is important for these contacts to be focused on group-related content only.
- Introduce the concept of ongoing assignments and/or home-based activities for the parents and their children. These activities should not be considered a chore but rather

a fun and necessary component to intervention. The assignments are intended to generalize what the parents and children are learning in the group to other settings such as home and school. Positive reinforcement can be used to enhance compliance (see the next section).

- Families will be encouraged to attend all weekly group sessions and will be asked to contact the group facilitators if they will be absent. They will be requested to have one consistent parent attend because alternating parents can disrupt the flow of the group as well as possibly impede understanding of therapeutic concepts. Every effort will be made to help families "catch up" when they miss a group session. Families will be asked to miss no more than 3 of the 14 scheduled sessions. An overview of the group intervention will be provided next session; parents are welcome to read the Intervention Overview before next group session if they wish.

Use of Reinforcement

Some of the children may be reluctant to attend group, separate from their parents to join the children's group, and/or try a new activity or learn a skill such as relaxation. Many times children benefit from an external motivator to participate until the activities themselves become inherently motivating. Not all families may feel comfortable using external rewards, but it is certainly an option for many families at the beginning of certain activities. The facilitators can support the parents in how to best use reinforcement throughout the course of the group, which may vary according to the needs of the individual child. It is extremely important to pair any external rewards with adult praise that recognizes that the child is being courageous and doing something that is hard for him or her. Parents can complete the Reinforcer Assessment worksheet to learn more about potential reinforcers for their children.

Completion of Parent Worksheets

Ask the parents to complete the Contact Information worksheet. Then, introduce the Brainstorming Goals! worksheet and have the parents either complete it in group or take it home (to discuss with a partner or spouse) and bring it back to the next group session. Facilitators will talk with parents about what they hope to get from the group. Emphasize that the primary focus of the group is on developing an awareness of anxiety symptoms in their children, developing a shared vocabulary for talking about anxiety symptoms and anxious events, and developing and implementing strategies for symptom reduction. As parents begin to generate goals for group, it may be important to have an initial discussion about realistic goals. For example, it is unlikely that all anxiety symptoms will be completely eliminated; instead, management of symptoms and decreased interference in day-to-day functioning may be more appropriate goals.

Helpful Hint As you help parents identify why they have come to group, you can emphasize that some of the concerns that parents may have about their children may actually be behavioral manifestations of anxiety symptoms. In this discussion, you are laying the foundation for parents to become good observers of their children's behavior and to begin to assess the extent to which previously described "oppositional" or "agitated" behavior may actually reflect anxiety symptoms. As with any group facilitation, it is important for the facilitators to provide opportunities for each family member to participate. For many parents, this may be the first opportunity that they have had to interact with other parents whose children may be similar to their own. Some parents may be highly verbal and, in their eagerness to share their stories, it may be difficult to highlight the core content of each session. It is your

(continued)

responsibility to structure each session in such a way that content is addressed while allowing for family information to be shared during group. Encouraging the parents to talk and form relationships with each other outside of group can be helpful to some families as well as to the group dynamic. Some parents may wish for the group to specifically improve their child's social skills. Discuss how attention to social skills is part of every session and that social skills are integrated into each target for intervention where appropriate. For example, if the goal is to talk to other children, the intervention plan will likely include focusing on increasing opportunities to talk to other children as well as identifying the necessary skills (e.g., initiating conversation, asking questions) for successfully talking with others.

Assignments

1. Complete the Brainstorming Goals! worksheet and bring it to the next session.
2. Bring back the Parent Workbook.

END—BACK TO LARGE GROUP

Contact Information

Name: _____

e-mail: _____

Home telephone: _____

Cell phone: _____

Work telephone: _____

My food allergies, if any (snack will be served during group):

_____

_____

My child's food allergies, if any (snack will be served during group):

_____

_____

Brainstorming Goals!

My goals for group:	My goals for my child for group:
1.	1.
2.	2.
3.	3.
4.	4.
5.	5.

Reinforcer Assessment

List the things that your child really enjoys under each category. Then, highlight the top 5 items/activities in categories that may motivate your child the most.

Foods and/or Drinks	Toys	Objects	Activities	People Your Child Enjoys
These may include video and electronic games, stuffed animals, movies, and so forth.	These may include sensory materials, household items, and so forth.	These may include outdoor activities or games (e.g., jumping on the trampoline), sensory activities (e.g., bath), and so forth.		

Child Group

Materials and/or Worksheets

- Written schedule
- Sticker cards and stickers
- Paper, pencils, pens, crayons, and markers
- Words for Worry Word Search worksheet

Goals

1. The children will learn to follow the routine for the group using a visual schedule.
2. The children will learn the rules for the group using a written list.
3. A sticker card system will be introduced, and children will learn to use the system.
4. Children will create cover drawings for their workbooks.
5. Children will generate a list of synonyms for the words *happy, mad, sad,* and *scared.*
6. Children will complete a worry word search.

Activities

1. *Written schedule:* The facilitator will post a written schedule on the wall, chalkboard, or a white board for each of the children's breakout sessions. The children can take turns crossing off the activities as they are completed.
2. *Rules for group:* For younger children in particular, it may be important to revisit the rules for group, and generate a brief list of rules that can be posted in the group room (e.g., listen to others when they are talking, compliment each other).
3. *Sticker program:* Each child will receive a card with his name on it and lots of space for stickers. The children will receive stickers when they display appropriate group behaviors. The target behaviors can include listening and helping others, ignoring inappropriate behaviors of other participants, and participating in group activities. Prizes will be given at the end of each group session. Because of the variability in behavior across participants, there is no minimum number of stickers necessary to earn a prize. You want to establish a positive atmosphere and reinforce appropriate group behaviors to prevent behavior management issues. The sticker cards may not be appropriate (or necessary) for older children. Group facilitators can make the determination about whether to use them, although it may be important to reward the children, regardless of age, with prizes at the end of group to reinforce good participation and effort.

Helpful Hint   It is important to strike a balance between giving the children stickers that are motivating and interesting to them and giving them stickers that are so motivating that they are distracting. Do not share the prize basket with the children until the end of the group session. The extent to which the sticker program is used and/or is necessary will vary. Feel free to use rewards other than stickers (e.g., small erasers, pencils, trading cards). Previous experience has indicated that the sticker program fades over time and is only minimally used by the end of the group sessions. Older children may not require or benefit from a sticker program, but experience has shown that small, age-appropriate prizes, even for older children, are well received.

4. *Cover drawings (Optional):* Ask the children to draw a picture on the inside back cover of their workbooks. They can include their name in the picture and share the picture with the group when everyone has finished. Encourage children who are reluctant to draw to write any distinguishing marks they choose on their paper. A number of children may prefer to write words rather than draw pictures.

Helpful Hint Feel free to schedule breaks throughout the children's group time. Some of the children may be able to handle the schedule as is, whereas others may need briefer periods of time focused on the activities with break time interspersed. Make a plan at the beginning of group so that the children know what to expect. Some of the children may need "fidget" toys. If so, you can gather together small objects that are okay for the children to play with during the breaks and perhaps even during some activities. Consider using a container for the fidget toys and/or other special-interest objects that the children may bring to group. You can build in time during the sessions for the children to play with their objects or toys. Write on the schedule when the down time or break will occur as a way to help the participants regroup and also decrease arousal. If the children require physical movement or other, more active, down time, feel free to schedule this in as well.

Helpful Hint Give all of the children a workbook, and ask them to bring the workbooks back and forth to the group. You should have extra workbooks and/or worksheets in case the children (or parents) lose them or leave them at home.

5. *Emotion words:* The purpose of this activity is for the children to generate a list of words that they use that are synonymous with the feeling words *happy, mad, sad,* and *scared.* Begin by dividing a large poster board into four main columns—one for each of the four main feeling words. The children may enjoy drawing faces to go with each of the feeling words. You can then have the children generate a long list of feeling words that you will write on a *separate* poster board and on index cards. Next, have the children place the index cards in the column with the feeling word that is most synonymous (e.g., *content* with *happy*). You can permanently post this poster board list of emotion words in the group room to increase the children's vocabulary of feeling words. If there is time, the children can complete the Words for Worry Word Search worksheet during group.

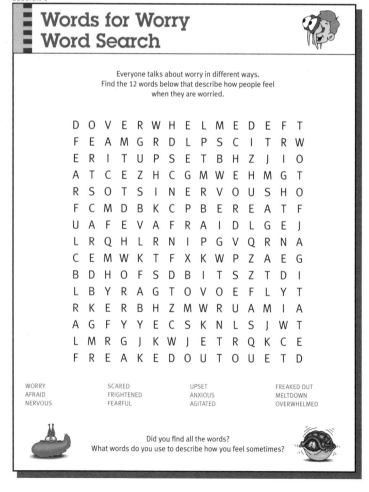

Assignments

1. The children can take home any incomplete work, including drawings for the covers of their workbooks.
2. The children can complete the word search by themselves or with their parents.
3. Bring back the workbooks.

END—BACK TO LARGE GROUP

▐▐▐▐▐▐ Large Group

(Children and Parents Together)

Materials and/or Worksheets

- Poster board for list of advice
- Prize basket

Activities

Closing/good-bye: For an ending ritual, have the children start and ultimately add to an ongoing list of coping strategies for handling worry, fear, and anxiety. These are strategies that the children or parents may already do (e.g., count to 10, tell themselves it will be okay, breathe deeply, read a favorite book, go for a walk), and you want to highlight these activities. Use a large sheet of poster board to keep track of the list of strategies shared by the children. If the children are not sure of what to say here, encourage the parents to offer suggestions on their child's behalf. Later in the intervention, you will compile the list of suggestions so that all of the children will have access to the "advice" of their friends. The children will be encouraged to post this list in their homes (e.g., bedroom walls, refrigerator). At the end of the first session, children can select a prize from the prize basket. Some children may take a long time to select a prize. If this is the case, feel free to give them a choice between two or three prizes.

END SESSION 1

Session Notes

_____

_____

_____

_____

_____

_____

_____

When I Worry

The purpose of Session 2 is to increase the ability of both the child and his parent or parents to identify and be aware of common anxiety symptoms that the child experiences. The children will begin to identify situations or things that make them worried or anxious. Children will expand their feeling and emotion vocabulary to learn to identify emotion words that tend to go with particular situations. The parent–child pairs (or trios) also will identify some of the behavioral or outward symptoms of anxiety—for example, how each child looks or behaves when anxious. Parents will begin to identify the steps involved in the cognitive behavior therapy (CBT) for anxiety. In addition, parent pairs or trios will continue to establish rapport with one another, both within the large group and in the parent and child breakout groups.

SESSION STRUCTURE

- Large group, children and parents together
- Parent–child pairs or trios
- Parent group and child group breakout sessions (occur simultaneously)
- Large group, children and parents together, for closing

SAMPLE SCHEDULE: WHEN I WORRY

- ■ **Large Group** (15–20 minutes)
  - Snack
  - Discussion about words for worry

- ■ **Parent–Child Pairs or Trios** (20–25 minutes)
  - What makes me worry?
  - What I look like when I worry

- ■ **Parent Group** (30–35 minutes)   ■ **Child Group** (30–35 minutes)
  - Emotion game
  - Storytime

- ■ **Large Group** (10 minutes)
  - Advice for friends
  - Prizes

SOCIAL SKILLS

- Greeting others; learning names of peers, parents, and facilitators
- Talking in front of a group

- Listening to others
- Asking questions and making comments
- Increasing emotion vocabulary and emotional expression
- Increasing awareness of nonverbal and/or verbal emotional expression (for self)
- Connecting different emotions to specific situations
- Providing information about events of the past week
- Listening to a reader during storytime

Suggestions for Supporting Social Skills

- Encourage effort and any approximation toward participation, but do not force.
- Provide verbal prompts. (These can be provided by parents and facilitators.)
- Model social skills.
- Use rewards for participation.

▦ Large Group (Children and Parents Together)

Materials and/or Worksheets

- Snacks
- Written schedule
- Written list of rules, posted on the wall if necessary
- Workbooks
- Words for Worry Word Search (from Session 1)

Goals

1. Children will state their favorite or preferred words for *happy, mad, sad,* and *scared.*
2. Children will state the words that they prefer to use as well as words they do not like to use for *worry.*[1]

> **Helpful Hint**   This is the first small activity that requires the children to have completed an assignment at home. It is important to have extra copies of the worksheets available and to remind parents to bring their and their child's workbooks back and forth. If this becomes a real problem, you can hold onto their workbooks and/or keep extra copies. Remember to reward the children for completing the assignment.

Activities

1. *Snacks:* Provide a variety of drinks and snack foods for parents and children when they arrive for group.
2. *Discussion:* Facilitators will review the activity from the previous week during which the children generated a list of emotion words. Remember that a primary purpose of this activity is to begin to establish a shared emotion vocabulary between parents and children. The following questions may be asked:

   - *Did everyone know the meaning of the words?*
   - *Which words were your favorite or preferred words for* happy, sad, mad, *or* scared?
   - *Which words best describe worry and/or anxiety for you?*

---

[1] A number of children in the group may be vehemently opposed to using certain words to describe worry; therefore, it is important to ask the children the words that they most prefer to describe anxiety or worry. Establishing a shared vocabulary between parents and children is important and begins here.

- *Are there words that you do not like or do not use?*
- *What words would you add?*

END—GROUP DIVIDES INTO PARENT–CHILD PAIRS OR TRIOS

Parent–Child Pairs or Trios

Materials and/or Worksheets

- Everybody Worries Sometimes worksheet
- How I React When I Worry worksheet
- This Is What I Look Like When I Worry worksheet
- Pens, pencils, crayons, and markers
- New sticker cards and stickers
- Group rules

Goals

1. Children will identify the situations or things that make them worry.
2. Children will describe and/or draw a picture of what worry and/or fear does to them.

Activities

1. *Completion of worksheets:* Parents and children will complete three main worksheets, time permitting. If they run out of time, they can finish the work at home and bring any one of the worksheets back next time. The three worksheets are 1) Everybody Worries Sometimes, 2) How I React When I Worry, and 3) This Is What I Look Like When I Worry. Begin with the Everybody Worries Sometimes worksheet and support pairs or trios as they complete their worksheets.

   - Everybody Worries Sometimes worksheet: Ask the children to work with their parent or parents to circle the items that make them worry. There will likely be disagreement between parents and children on some of the items, so it is important for the children and parents to create separate lists; the purpose of the task is to increase the child's self-awareness of what makes him or her worry, even if he or she and his or her parent do not agree. In introducing this worksheet, the facilitator might note the following:

     For this activity, it is important to select fears or worries that truly interfere with day-to-day functioning. For example, most of us might say we are worried or afraid of tornados, but this worry would interfere with our daily lives only *if the worry prevented us from going outside on cloudy days, prevented us from sitting near windows if there was a dark cloud in the sky, or made us feel very scared even if the tornado was spotted many miles away. If you select a large number of worries, then please highlight the five worries that interfere most with your day-to-day functioning.*

   - How I React When I Worry worksheet: Ask the children to identify what worry does to them—what they look like or how someone else might be able to tell when they are worried.
   - This Is What I Look Like When I Worry worksheet: Ask the children to draw a picture of what they look like when they worry.

2. *Share time:* When the pairs have completed the worksheets, encourage the children to share their worksheets with one other pair. (If appropriate, share time can occur in the large group instead.)

Helpful Hints   These worksheets may be quite difficult for the children and their parents, particularly the Everybody Worries Sometimes worksheet. The children may not want to admit or acknowledge their anxieties or symptoms they may perceive as embarrassing. In addition, the children may not be aware of their anxieties or worries, leading the parents—who are acutely aware of their children's difficulties—to feel frustrated that their children are not accurately identifying their anxious thoughts or situations that make them anxious. Therefore, it is important to use this activity as a way to begin the dialogue around worry and events that trigger worry or anxiety. Developing a shared vocabulary of worry may take a number of weeks to establish. The list that the children generate is not intended to be comprehensive of all of their worries or anxiety symptoms. Parents will need to help their children generate ideas over time and identify situations that may cause them worry. If parents disagree with their child's selections, have them mark their perceptions of their child's worries in a different-color pen rather than trying to change their child's ratings.

    The children may not want to share ideas with their friends, but try to encourage a bit of sharing because other group members will likely share some of their worries. It is an essential part of the group that the children learn that others share similar worries and problems.

    Support the group work between parent and child, with the therapists positioned more peripherally. Parents need to learn to talk effectively with their children, even when they disagree and/or are frustrated. During this activity, some children may interpret "When I worry I do this" as an opportunity to generate coping strategies. If that is the case, you can commend them for generating ideas on how to cope and encourage them to record these ideas in their workbooks in the notes section for future reference.

END—GROUP DIVIDES INTO PARENT GROUP AND CHILD GROUP

Sometimes it can be hard to think about what makes us feel worried. Together with your mom or dad, think about what things make you worry or feel nervous. Then, look at the Everybody Worries Sometimes worksheet on the next page. Maybe you'll find something you worry about on that list. Feel free to add worries if you do not see them. Remember, *everybody* worries sometimes, even adults.

Everybody Worries Sometimes

Kids *and* adults worry.

People worry about. . .

- ❏ Storms and/or tornados
- ❏ Dogs and/or cats
- ❏ Letting go of past events
- ❏ Being late
- ❏ Bugs, spiders, and/or bees
- ❏ The dark
- ❏ Getting to sleep
- ❏ Talking to new people
- ❏ Being away from family
- ❏ Being home alone
- ❏ Using public bathrooms
- ❏ Getting a disease
- ❏ Making mistakes
- ❏ Going to someone's house
- ❏ Starting homework
- ❏ Trying new foods
- ❏ _____
- ❏ _____
- ❏ _____

- ❏ Being in a room by myself
- ❏ World events
- ❏ Being teased
- ❏ Loud noises
- ❏ Heights
- ❏ Starting a conversation
- ❏ Parents going out
- ❏ Germs
- ❏ Asking for help
- ❏ Dying
- ❏ Getting lost
- ❏ Scary movies
- ❏ Lots of people
- ❏ Talking in school
- ❏ Changes
- ❏ Performing in front of others

Do you worry about any of these things?
Think about how much these worries bother you each day.

Kids do different things when they get worried. Some kids get really quiet. Other kids get restless and have a hard time sitting still. Sometimes, it's hard to recognize what we do when we get nervous. Together with your mom or dad, think and talk about how your body reacts when you worry or feel nervous.

After talking with your mom or dad, circle on the How I React When I Worry worksheet how your body reacts when you worry. Highlight your five most common reactions to worry.

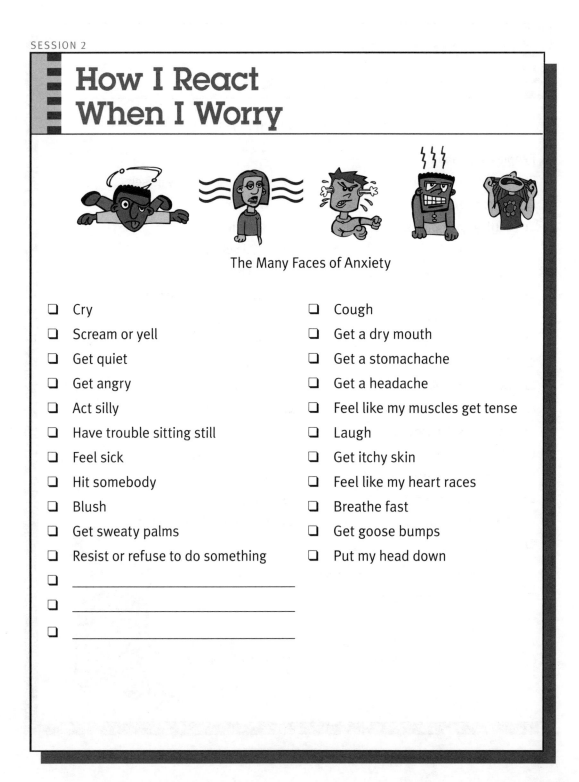

How I React When I Worry

The Many Faces of Anxiety

❏ Cry

❏ Scream or yell

❏ Get quiet

❏ Get angry

❏ Act silly

❏ Have trouble sitting still

❏ Feel sick

❏ Hit somebody

❏ Blush

❏ Get sweaty palms

❏ Resist or refuse to do something

❏ _____

❏ _____

❏ _____

❏ Cough

❏ Get a dry mouth

❏ Get a stomachache

❏ Get a headache

❏ Feel like my muscles get tense

❏ Laugh

❏ Get itchy skin

❏ Feel like my heart races

❏ Breathe fast

❏ Get goose bumps

❏ Put my head down

On the This Is What I Look Like When I Worry worksheet on next page, draw a picture of what you look like when you worry. Talk with your mom or dad, and look at the list you just made about what you do when you worry. This will help you to think about how to draw your picture.

This Is What I Look Like When I Worry

▌▌▌▌▌▌ Parent Group

Materials and/or Worksheets

- Brainstorming Goals! worksheet
- Intervention Overview worksheet

Goals

1. Parents will share goals and/or objectives for the group.
2. Parents will identify the steps involved in the intervention for anxiety symptoms as well as identify their role in the treatment process.

Activities

1. *Discussion:* Include the following in main points and/or activities to structure the discussion.

- Answer any logistical questions such as scheduling or the communication process among parents or between parents and facilitators.
- Ask parents to share with the group their completed Brainstorming Goals! worksheets from the previous session.
- Using the Intervention Overview worksheet, begin to provide an overview of the intervention program and what it may look like for the children in the group. The Intervention Overview worksheet can be summarized as follows:

   1. Assist children in gaining self-awareness of anxiety symptoms and how they may present, identifying and labeling anxiety-provoking and/or fearful situations.
   2. Establish a framework for thinking about anxiety. For example, anxiety is a problem of over-reactivity. Some bodies overreact to lots of different situations, signaling danger when there is no real danger. Children and parents will learn to differentiate real danger from "false alarms."
   3. Establish a stimulus hierarchy of fearful situations—in other words, short, graded steps that illustrate how to face fears a little at a time.
   4. Review social skills (see below).
   5. Generate tools including strategies for calming the body and the mind (e.g., relaxation and other calming activities, positive self-statements or "helpful thoughts").
   6. Use graded exposure (facing fears a little at a time) to show the children and parents that they can handle their anxious feelings.
   7. Give children "stress-o-meters" to record and/or monitor anxiety on a daily basis and to use during exposure sessions.
   8. Have children and parents select a target fear or worry and make a plan for facing the fear and implementing tools to decrease the worry and/or anxious feelings.
   9. Reward children for facing their fears.

- Discuss social skills. There is not a specific social skills module included in this intervention package, but opportunities to identify and teach social skills occur throughout each session. For example, greeting others, sharing personal information in a group, listening to others, asking questions, and making appropriate comments are a few of the social skills that children work on during every session. It also is important to directly teach essential social skills while identifying steps for facing fears. For example, if a child identifies a fear of talking to peers, then it would be important to teach the child a basic social skill set necessary to talk to peers (e.g., how to start a conversation, how to end a conversation, paying attention to basic nonverbal behaviors) in addition to developing a stimulus hierarchy for facing his or her fear of starting a conversation with another child.

- Provide an overview of the parent component to treatment, emphasizing the parent's role as a coach (Barrett et al., 2004; Cobham et al., 1998; Mendlowitz et al., 1999). This role includes the following:

    1. Convey empathy about your child's feelings of fear, worry, and/or anxiety.
    2. Express encouragement and confidence in your child's abilities to face his or her fears.
    3. Model courageous behavior. (Pick a time when you are feeling anxious and narrate how you are going to get through it.)
    4. Encourage brave behaviors and help your child practice facing his or her fears by using graded exposure techniques.
    5. Help your child to make the connection between thoughts and feelings and how these emotions make his or her body feel.
    6. Reward courageous behavior.
    7. Ignore excessive displays of anxiety.
    8. Learn to recognize parental anxiety and/or parenting style factors that may unintentionally increase anxiety in your child or expose him or her to fearful situations.
    9. Establish a plan for sharing treatment information with your spouse and/or partner.

Helpful Hint The purpose of going over the Intervention Overview worksheet is to familiarize the parents with the treatment approach early on in the intervention. The parents may not fully understand all of the components immediately, but this exercise is intended as an introduction to the treatment. You will repeatedly review the steps in the intervention throughout group. You can tie together the work the parents did in pairs earlier in the session, highlighting that they worked on the initial step of identifying anxiety symptoms and corresponding situations that make their children anxious.

END—BACK TO LARGE GROUP

Intervention Overview

Below, you will see a brief summary of the treatment approach for anxiety and what the main topics are for discussion in the upcoming weeks. This treatment overview may look rather intimidating at first; keep in mind, however, that we will be reviewing and discussing these concepts repeatedly throughout the group sessions.

1. Identify symptoms of anxiety and situations or things that make your child anxious.

    - By identifying the variety of symptoms of anxiety your child displays when he or she is worried or fearful, you are teaching self-awareness of symptoms and behaviors. Later, when you observe these behaviors, you can coach your child to use the coping strategies and tools practiced in group sessions.

    - By identifying the situations that make your child anxious or the objects, places, or people that your child avoids, you will be able to get a sense of what contributes to your child's anxiety as well as how much these symptoms affect your lives. The identification of these situations also will become the foundation for creating exposure hierarchies, or in other words, facing fears gradually (see number 6).

2. Establish a context for thinking about anxiety.

    - Physical reactions to anxiety: Anxiety is a problem of overreactivity. When you sense or feel real danger, such as when you are in a burning building, your body goes into action—fight, flight, or freeze. Some people's bodies, however, overreact to lots of different situations, signaling danger when there is no real danger. Physical reactions such as dry mouth, rapid heart rate, and sweaty palms may continue despite the "false alarm." Self-awareness of these "false alarms" will be emphasized along with strategies to reduce the body's physical reaction as well as to change your child's beliefs about the event.

    - Externalize anxiety: You and your child, together with the group facilitators, will fight his or her anxiety symptoms. The children will create "worry bugs" to represent worry or fear. The children will then identify friends and family members on their team who will help them beat anxiety. Your child's success depends on our joint efforts!

3. Introduce tools or strategies to fight or resist anxiety symptoms.

    - Get a handle on the body's physical reaction: Work to decrease anxiety with deep breathing or by engaging in other calming activities. Your child will practice measuring and monitoring anxiety symptoms in a regular way; as the children increase awareness of anxiety symptoms and corresponding strategies for relaxing or calming themselves, they are developing skills to improve emotion regulation.

    - Pay attention to "active minds" or thoughts that tend to occur when your child is worried or fearful, and help your child generate "helpful" thoughts instead.

    - Encourage a plan for self-evaluation and/or self-reward.

4. Identify and teach necessary social skills.

    - There is not a specific social skills module included in this intervention package, but opportunities to identify and teach social skills occur throughout each session. In addition, if it appears as though social skills deficits may be exacerbating your child's anxiety in a particular situation, the necessary social skills will be taught through role play and scripting, along with graded exposure techniques.

(continued)

(continued)
Intervention Overview

5. Determine your child's steps to success.

   - You and your child will list many of the objects, places, or people that make your child anxious and rank order them based on how much anxiety they produce and/or how much they interfere with your child's quality of life. You will then select a starting point and work to gradually have your child face his or her fears.

6. Help your child make a plan to face his or her fears.

   - Choose a reasonable, low-intensity target.

   - Identify tools and/or strategies that your child finds most effective in reducing anxiety symptoms.

   - Practice during group sessions and at home, gradually facing fears (exposure hierarchy).

7. Encourage self-evaluation and self-reward as a final step in facing fears.

   - Teach your child to evaluate his or her own behavior. Rate his or her effort in handling anxiety-producing situations and identify strategies for what he or she could do differently the next time. Parents may reward children for their effort in facing fears, and children ultimately can be taught to reward themselves.

8. Prevent relapse of symptoms by reviewing and practicing coping techniques, establishing plans for handling future symptoms, and taking home the *Facing Your Fears* group videos made by the children.

9. Try these additional recommendations (Barrett et al., 2004; Cobham et al., 1998; Mendlowitz et al., 1999).

   - Encourage and reward your child for his or her effort and engagement in brave behaviors.

   - Ignore excessive displays of anxiety.

   - Make the connection between anxious thoughts, physical changes your child may experience, and anxious behaviors.

   - Convey confidence in your child's ability to handle his or her worry and/or anxiety.

   - Model your own courageous behaviors.

   - Be aware of your parenting style and/or any personal anxiety issues that may affect your child's ability to face fears.

   - Work together with your spouse and/or partner to develop a plan.

   - Remember, we may learn best from the mistakes we make (Kendall & Hedtke, 2006).

▌▌▌▌▌ Child Group

Materials and/or Worksheets

- Emotion cards and situations; examples can be found on the Suggested Emotion Words and Related Situations worksheet
- *Alicia Has a Bad Day* (Jahn-Clough, 1994); *Alexander and the Terrible, Horrible, No Good, Very Bad Day* (Viorst, 1987); or other similar storybooks

Goals

1. Children will expand feeling or emotion vocabulary by participating in a number of activities.
2. Children will accurately match a correct feeling word to a particular situation and identify *why* someone might feel a certain way.

Activities

1. *Emotion game:* Write down on index cards potential situations that may elicit fear, anxiety, or other emotions. The Suggested Emotion Words and Related Situations worksheet lists a number of potential situations such as *John forgets his homework at home* or *Stephanie lost her favorite video game.* Write emotion words on index cards also; these words may include *happy, mad, sad, scared, embarrassed, afraid, silly, amused, nervous,* and so forth. Feel free to add emotion words and/or situations. Taking turns, have each child select a card and identify possible emotions. For example, a child may read the card *Daniel has a test in spelling tomorrow.* You may then ask, "How does he feel?" Some children may wish to act out the emotions or situations. After the other children identify the emotion portrayed, one of the children can offer additional suggestions for *why* someone might feel specific emotions in that situation. For children who choose multiple emotions for each situation, have them select the *best* one or two emotion words. Reward their efforts with stickers for participation. The primary purpose of this activity is to expand the children's emotion vocabulary *and* to tie emotions to situations. We intentionally include emotions that are unrelated to worry and anxiety because focusing solely on these emotions may be too much for some children. There is no need to complete all 12 situations. It may be helpful to choose fewer situations but allow for a more in-depth discussion on those situations and the emotions they elicit. Older children may prefer to generate personal situations rather than use the examples provided on the worksheet.
2. *Storytime:* If storytime is appropriate (younger children typically enjoy this!) you may read *Alicia Has a Bad Day* (Jahn-Clough, 1994) or *Alexander and the Terrible, Horrible, No Good, Very Bad Day* (Viorst, 1987) or any other similar book. These books talk about feeling badly but also finding appropriate ways to handle negative emotions. This is an optional activity. If this activity seems too young for older children, then you may eliminate this activity.

Children's Assignments

1. Complete any unfinished worksheets.
2. Bring workbooks back.

END—BACK TO LARGE GROUP

Suggested Emotion Words and Related Situations

Emotion words

Mad	Sad	Silly	Bored
Scared	Happy	Excited	Calm
Frightened	Worried	Surprised	Brave
Amused	Embarrassed	Upset	

Situations

1. John forgets his homework at home.

2. Sasha just found out that her younger sister broke her favorite toy.

3. Derek's birthday is tomorrow.

4. Isabel just took a walk with her dog, and her body feels relaxed.

5. Carlos did a math problem in front of the class and made a mistake.

6. Stephanie lost her favorite video game.

7. Erik's vacation is over and he has to go to school tomorrow.

8. Lily's teacher told a funny story in class.

9. Daniel has a test in spelling tomorrow.

10. Ella's brother yelled, "boo!" as she went down the hall.

11. Michael is going to see a Star Wars movie tonight.

12. Abby is normally afraid of dogs, but when she saw her friend walking her dog, she asked to pet it.

▌▌▌▌▌ Large Group (Children and Parents Together)

Activity

1. *Closing/good-bye:* Continue with advice poster, and give children prizes for sticker cards.

END SESSION 2

Session Notes

_____

_____

_____

_____

_____

_____

_____

_____

_____

_____

_____

_____

_____

_____

_____

_____

_____

_____

_____

_____

Time Spent Worrying

The purpose of Session 3 is to have the children visually indicate how much time they spend worrying now and how much time they *predict* that they will spend worrying after treatment. They also will identify activities that they would spend more time doing if they did not have to spend so much time worrying or feeling anxious. In this session, worry is externalized, or separated out, from the children (March & Mulle, 1998). That is, rather than considering anxiety symptoms an inevitable part of a child's life, we emphasize that anxiety symptoms can be a separate entity— anthropomorphized in such a way that the child and others can fight or resist giving in to the symptoms. The children are supported by their team (i.e., parents, therapists, peers) as they resist their worries. In the parent group, parents will continue to discuss the treatment approach and their role in their children's treatment. Parents also will discuss the ways that *they* relax so that they can be prepared to help their children engage in calming and relaxing activities in an ongoing way.

SESSION STRUCTURE

- Large group, children and parents together
- Parent–child pairs or trios
- Parent group and child group breakout sessions (occur simultaneously)
- Large group, children and parents together, for closing

SAMPLE SCHEDULE: TIME SPENT WORRYING

- **Large Group** (15 minutes)
  - Snack
  - Discussion—review of schedule

- **Parent–Child Pairs or Trios** (20–25 minutes)
  - Time spent worrying now
  - Time spent worrying in the future
  - When worry goes away, I'll…
  - Share time

- **Parent Group** (40 minutes)

- **Child Group** (40 minutes)
  - Worry bugs and helper bugs
  - My team (people that will help me)
  - Squashing my worry bug!
  - Game: All About Me!
  - Show-and-Tell Planning

■ **Large Group** (10 minutes)
- Advice for friends
- Prizes

SOCIAL SKILLS

- Greeting others by name
- Sharing personal information in front of a group
- Increasing understanding about anxiety-provoking situations
- Listening to others
- Opportunities to compliment each other's work (worry bugs/helper bugs)
- Asking questions and making comments during share time and All About Me game

Suggestions for Supporting Social Skills

- Encourage effort and any approximation toward participation, but do not force.
- Provide verbal and/or visual (use worksheets) prompts. (These can be provided by parents and facilitators.)
- Model social skills.
- Use rewards for participation.

▪▪▪▪▪▪ Large Group (Children and Parents Together)

Materials and/or Worksheets

- Snacks
- Written schedule
- Written list of rules, posted on the wall if necessary
- Treatment manuals

Goals

1. Children will go over the schedule for the day and have a snack.

Activities

1. *Snack:* Provide a variety of drinks and snack foods for parents and children when they arrive for group.
2. *Discussion:* Introduction to the day—review the schedule and ask if there are any questions before the group splits into parent–child pairs or trios.

END—GROUP DIVIDES INTO PARENT–CHILD PAIRS OR TRIOS

▪▪▪▪▪▪ Parent–Child Pairs or Trios

Materials and/or Worksheets

- Group of worksheets for teaching the concept of time spent worrying
- How Much Time Do You Spend Worrying Now? worksheet
- How Much Time Do You Predict You Will Spend Worrying in the Future? worksheet
- When Worry Goes Away, I'll… worksheet

Goals

1. Children will complete several introductory worksheets visually depicting how much time other children may spend worrying.
2. Children will identify how much time out of their day they spend worrying by completing the How Much Time Do You Spend Worrying Now? worksheet with their parents.
3. Children will indicate how much of their day they predict they will spend worrying in the future (after treatment) by completing the How Much Time Do You Predict You Will Spend Worrying in the Future? worksheet with their parents.
4. The children also will make a list of activities that they would like to do when their anxiety and worries are reduced or go away.

Activities

1. *Worksheets*

   - A packet of worksheets will introduce the concept of how much time people may spend worrying. There are several different worksheets that visually depict cartoon children "thinking" about their worries. The worries are listed in bubbles next to each cartoon child, and the children in the group are asked to match the amount of time the cartoon child spends worrying with the amount and intensity of the child's fears. Note that intensity of worry is important to consider, and remind the children of the following:

   Time spent worrying is determined by the number of things people worry about as well as the intensity of the worry. More time spent worrying means less time doing fun things.[1]

   The parent–child pairs or trios may want to refer back to the Everybody Worries Sometimes worksheet if they are having a hard time completing this packet.

   - Once the children understand the concept of visually depicting their anxiety, they will use the How Much Time Do You Spend Worrying Now? worksheet to list their own worries (selecting worries that truly interfere with daily functioning), denote how intense their worry is, and determine how much of their day they spend worrying.
   - Next, ask the children to use the How Much Time Do You Predict You Will Spend Worrying in the Future? worksheet to *predict* the amount of time they will spend worrying in the future (after treatment).
   - Finally, using the When Worry Goes Away, I'll… worksheet, the children will write down the activities they would like to engage in rather than wasting their time worrying.

2. *Share time:* As in previous sessions, when the pairs have completed the forms, encourage the children to share their worksheets with the other group members.

Helpful Hint   Parents and children may disagree about the amount of time the child spends worrying. If this is the case, parents and children can complete separate diagrams. The idea is to help parents and children begin to agree on the worry symptoms and how much the symptoms interfere with the children's day-to-day functioning. Do not force them to agree, but rather appreciate that they may have a difference of opinion. Some children may be able to complete the Worry in the Future worksheet with no problem, whereas others may have more difficulty; as with a number of concepts discussed in this manual, it is important to introduce the worksheet to the children but not insist on completion. The goal of this activity, in part, is to create motivation for change and communicate that time spent worrying is wasted time.

END—GROUP DIVIDES INTO PARENT GROUP AND CHILD GROUP

---

[1]For this activity, it is not necessary to be exact in the amount of time that the children worry but rather to convey the concept that worry can interfere with their ability to have fun and often can be wasted time. Help the children discern repetitive worrying from time spent problem-solving about their worries, because problem-solving can be productive.

Now you are going to look at how much time you spend worrying during the day.

On the next pages, you are going to read about Michael, Annie, and John. They are kids your age who spend time worrying during the day. One of them worries a lot, one of them worries sometimes, and one of them does not spend much time worrying at all.

Together with your mom or dad, figure out how much time they each spend worrying.

After you read about Michael, Annie, and John, you are going to think about how much time *you* spend worrying *now*. Then, you will predict how much time you think you'll spend worrying in the *future*, once you learn to handle your worry.

Start reading about Michael, Annie, and John on the next pages.

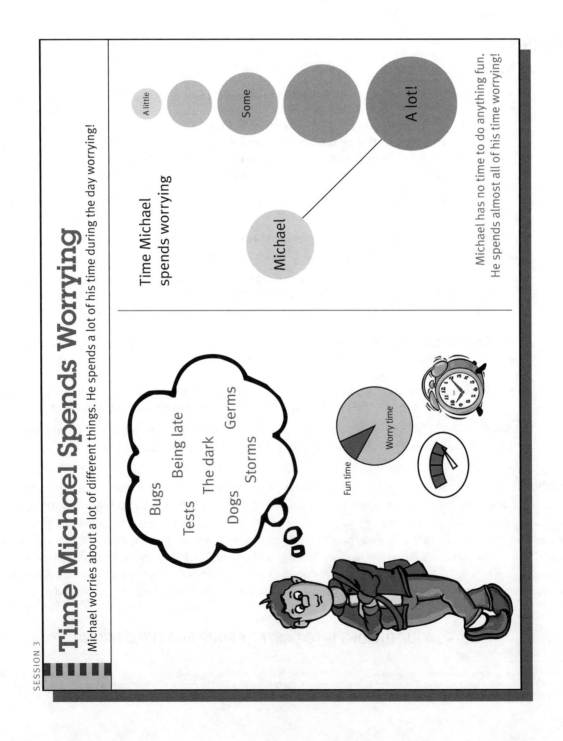

Time Annie Spends Worrying

Annie sometimes gets nervous about tests, and she is a little scared of big storms.
How much time do you think she spends worrying?

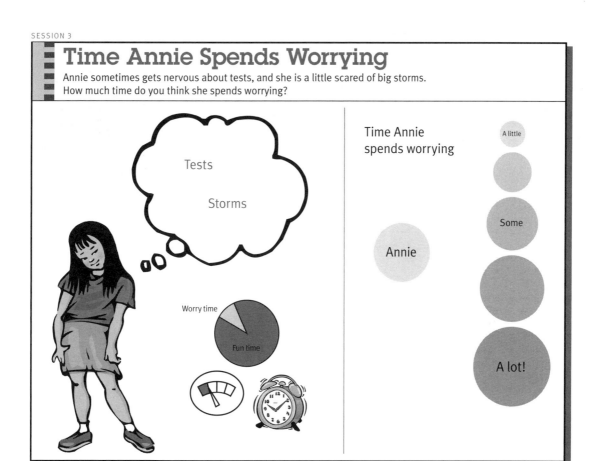

Time John Spends Worrying

John worries about tests, homework, making mistakes, and being late.
How much time do you think he spends worrying?

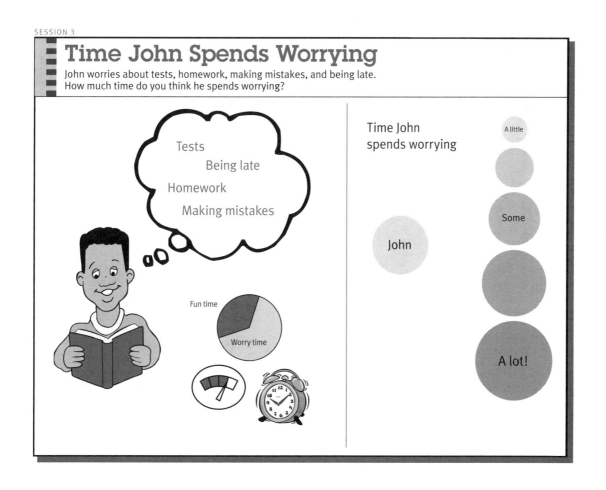

How Much Time Do You Spend Worrying Now?

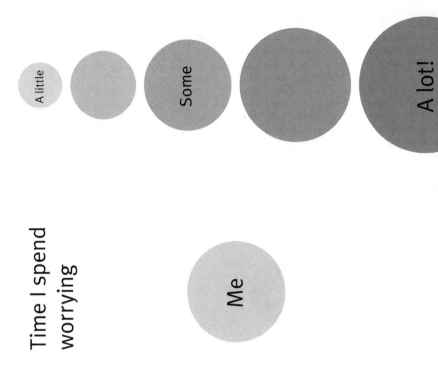

Time I spend worrying

Me

Some

A little

A lot!

Write down your worries here!

Fun time

Worry time

How Much Time Do You Predict You Will Spend Worrying in the Future?

When Worry Goes Away, I'll...

Write what you will spend your time doing
in the future when you no longer worry as much.

1. _____

2. _____

3. _____

4. _____

5. _____

Or draw!

▌▌▌▌▌ Parent Group

Materials and/or Worksheets

- Intervention Overview worksheet (from Session 2)
- Things I Like to Do to Relax worksheet

Goals

1. Parents will review the steps involved in the intervention program for anxiety symptoms.

Activities

1. *Discussion*

   - Finish reviewing the Intervention Overview worksheet as well as parent recommendations for intervention, and answer any questions. As you review the treatment components today as well as in future sessions, it may be important to have the parents role-play some of the concepts to make sure that they feel comfortable supporting these concepts at home. Role plays may be particularly helpful if a parent predicts that her child will have a difficult reaction to some of the activities.
   - Review what the children will be doing in their small group. Emphasize the following:

     It is important for parents to know what the children will cover in small group so that they can reinforce the concepts that are introduced. A review of the children's groups will happen every week.

   - At this time, review the children's worksheets and indicate that the primary purpose behind all of these worksheets (e.g., Worry Bug, Helper Bug) is to imagine that the worry and/or anxiety symptoms are separate from the children (March & Mulle, 1998). In addition, emphasize that the children will identify a team of support including parents, other family members, friends, the group facilitators, peers in the group, and even fictional characters to help them fight worry. Then, children will play the "All About Me" game (an informal game where the children learn more about each other; see Child Group section for more information) and plan Show and Tell—both activities designed to help them highlight their strengths and/or interests. Parents can encourage the children to engage in these activities rather than spend wasted time on worry and/or anxiety. These activities all provide suggestions for how the children could spend their time when their worry time has decreased.
   - Preview for next week. Let parents know that during the next session you will be talking about relaxation and calming activities. To help children brainstorm about relaxation and engage in relaxing or calming activities, parents can begin thinking about how *they* relax. Ask parents to talk about their own experiences with anxiety and anxiety-provoking situations. They can be encouraged to talk about how they handle anxiety themselves, what they do on a regular basis to relax, and what they do when their own "false alarms" go off. Provide examples of how parents can talk through their own stress (e.g., "I'm feeling really stressed right now; I'm going to take a couple deep breaths") to provide a good coping model for their child. Parents can be encouraged to share these examples with their children.
   - Things I Like to Do to Relax worksheet: Parents will be asked to generate a number of different activities that they engage in *on a regular basis* that they find calming and relaxing. They also can include activities that are particularly helpful to them when they are stressed. Encourage the parents to share the list with the other participants. As the parents highlight the things that they do on a daily basis to help themselves relax and/

or engage in when they are anxious or stressed, they may be better able to help their children generate ideas for calming activities of their own. This group session emphasizes relaxation and regular use of calming activities for *both* parents and children because although some adults may naturally take relaxation breaks, many children (and some adults) need to be taught specifically the importance of engaging in daily and portable calming strategies.

Parent's Assignments:

1.   Remind children to bring any objects they may need for Show and Tell.

END—BACK TO LARGE GROUP

SESSION 3

Things I Like to Do to Relax

We all engage in a number of different relaxing or calming activities in our day-to-day lives. Sometimes, these activities help us calm down when we are feeling particularly stressed or anxious. Today, we will spend a little time sharing some of these ideas. Your child just learned about several children and how much time they spend worrying. With these activities fresh in your mind, you may better be able to help your child generate some calming and/or relaxing activities that might work for him or her on a daily basis when he or she is feeling stressed or anxious. First, take a little time to jot down some things you do to relax on this form.

_____

_____

_____

_____

_____

_____

_____

_____

_____

_____

_____

_____

_____

_____

◀▐▐▐▐ Child Group

Materials and/or Worksheets

- My Worry Bug worksheet
- My Helper Bug worksheet
- My Team worksheet
- Squashing My Worry Bug! worksheet
- Pencils, pens, crayons, markers, paper, and scissors
- Set of different-colored Play-Doh or clay
- Bowl for selecting of interests
- Digital camera

Goals

1. Children will name and create their worry bugs.
2. Children will create a helper bug and/or a representation of themselves "squashing" their worry bugs.
3. Children will identify a team of people who will help them fight or resist worry.
4. Children will identify up to five favorite interests for themselves and the other group members.
5. Children will plan for Show and Tell to share for next session.

Activities

1. Worry bugs and helper bugs

   Almost everyone has a "worry bug." When we experience worry (i.e., anxiety, fear, or distress) and cannot make it go away, it may be that our worry bugs are getting in our way. These feelings make it hard for us to learn in school, have fun at home, or play with our friends. Sometimes worry can be a little problem; sometimes it may be a big problem. In this activity, you will draw your own worry bugs and give them names. You can draw your bugs on the My Worry Bug worksheet.

   - Some children may prefer to mold their worry bug from clay or Play-Doh. After children have created their worry bugs, take pictures with a digital camera to give to the children at the next session.

   Now, draw or create a "helper bug"—an imaginary creature (e.g., based on a fictional character or the child's own creation) that helps you "beat" your worry bug. You can draw or mold your helper bugs on the My Helper Bug worksheet.

   - Clay or Play-Doh will be available for children who prefer using these materials over drawing. Again, use the camera to take a picture of the child's helper bug.
   - My Team worksheet: Here, the children can list the people (real or imagined) who can help them fight worry. You can suggest that they include parents, other family members, friends, group facilitators, peers from the group, or fictional characters.
   - After these worksheets have been completed, ask the children to draw a picture on the Squashing My Worry Bug! worksheet of herself (and her team) squashing the worry bug. Children who made clay bugs can literally squash their bugs. Again, digital photos can be taken and given out at the next session.
   - Share time: Remember to build in share time after the children have completed the tasks. Informal sharing may occur during these activities, but if not, encourage children to show each other their work.

2. *All About Me game:* To support the children in engaging in positive activities, highlight their individual strengths, and learn more about each other they will play the game "All About Me." To play, have the children write down on separate pieces of paper up to five favorite interests or fun facts about themselves. Next, put these pieces of paper in a bowl and have the children select an item, one at a time, and guess who wrote each interest.

3. *Show-and-Tell planning:* Encourage the children to bring in an example of a particular personal interest or activity to share with the large group next week, again to emphasize the importance of engaging in activities other than worry. This activity is especially popular with younger children, although older children may want to share their special interests as well. Show and Tell may be scheduled on a regular basis at the end of each group session if there is interest. Initially, all of the children can briefly share their interests during each group session; however, if this activity becomes of great interest to the children, then the facilitators may want to alternate presentations (e.g., have only one or two presentations per group). An additional benefit of having a Show and Tell period is that it allows children to forge friendships over common interests and to practice appropriate social skills (e.g., doing a brief presentation, answering questions). The children also typically look forward to sharing their special interests with the group, which serves as an additional motivator for coming to group.

Helpful Hint   The primary purpose of having the children complete the worry bug set of worksheets is to externalize their anxiety symptoms and build the thinking that they can fight or beat their worry and/or anxiety. As with previous activities, some children may refuse to participate in the worry bug activities. Alternative activities may be offered, especially for older children; however, our experience has been that most of the children in the group, regardless of age, have enjoyed this activity. Our approach thus far has been to support the children in this process and not force them to do something that they cannot do at present. Feel free to be creative and offer the children options for participation that maintain the spirit of the activity!

Assignments

1. Plan for Show and Tell, and bring any objects necessary for the next session.
2. Finish worksheets that were not completed.

END—BACK TO LARGE GROUP

Next, you are going to create several characters. Your first character is your WORRY BUG. Almost everyone has a worry bug. Worry bugs are the fears and anxiety that get in our way and make it hard for us to learn in school, have fun at home, or play with friends.

What does your worry bug look like?
What will you call it?

Once you have drawn or created your worry bug on the next page, draw or create your HELPER BUG. A helper bug is an imaginary creature that helps you defeat your worry bug!

What does your helper bug look like?
What will you call it?

Next, write the names of all of the friends, family members, or fictional characters (your team) that can help you beat worry!

Finally, create something (either with Play-Doh or markers) that shows you and your helper bug squashing your worry bug!

My Team to Help Beat Worry

Squashing My Worry Bug!

▌▌▌▌▌ Large Group (Children and Parents Together)

Activity

1. *Closing/good-bye:* Continue with advice poster, and give children prizes for their sticker cards. Remind parents and children of the plan for Show and Tell and remind them to bring their materials next session.

    Note: Stress-o-meters will be used in Session 4, and each child will need one, so all necessary materials will need to be gathered prior to the next session.

END SESSION 3

Session Notes

_____

_____

_____

_____

_____

_____

_____

_____

_____

_____

_____

_____

_____

_____

_____

_____

What Worry Does to My Body

Beginning to Measure Worry

The purpose of Session 4 is to talk about how our bodies react or feel when we are anxious. We will discuss the range of physical feelings that people can experience when they are anxious, as well as work on increasing awareness of the body's worry reactions. Thus, handling our body's reaction to anxiety is a focus of this session. Children will be taught calming and/or relaxing activities and will identify additional calming activities that they can do at home to help with emotion regulation. Also in this session, the children will receive their "stress-o-meters" for measuring anxiety, personalize them, and begin to learn how to use them.

SESSION STRUCTURE

- Large group, children and parents together
- Parent–child pairs or trios
- Large group, children and parents together

SAMPLE SCHEDULE: WHAT WORRY DOES TO MY BODY

- **Large Group** (25–30 minutes)
  - Snack
  - Discussion: Review of schedule and check in with Show and Tell
  - The body's reaction to worry and/or fear
  - Video

- **Parent–Child Pairs or Trios** (45–50 minutes)
  - Deep breathing
  - What I like to do to relax
  - Measuring anxiety—introduction to stress-o-meters
  - Share time

- **Large Group** (10–15 minutes)
  - Show and Tell
  - Deep breathing
  - Prizes

SOCIAL SKILLS

- Greeting others by name
- Sharing personal information in front of a group

- Increasing understanding of anxiety-provoking situations and corresponding physical reactions
- Listening to others
- Asking questions and making comments during Show and Tell

Suggestions for Supporting Social Skills

- Encourage effort and any approximation toward participation, but do not force.
- Provide verbal and/or visual (use worksheets) prompts. (These can be provided by parents and facilitators.)
- Model social skills.
- Use rewards for participation.

▚▚▚ Large Group (Children and Parents Together)

Materials and/or Worksheets

- Snacks
- Written schedule
- Written list of rules, posted on the wall if necessary
- Pencils and/or markers
- What Worry Does to Your Body worksheet
- *Facing Your Fears* video on relaxation training (included on the accompanying DVD)

Goals

1. Children will identify and share with the group (as long as they feel comfortable) at least three physical reactions to anxiety.
2. Children will define worry's "false alarm," indicating that they understand that sometimes our bodies have physiological reactions that are really "false alarms"; at these times, no real danger is present.

Activities

1. *Snack:* Provide a variety of drinks and snack foods for parents and children when they arrive for group.
2. *Show-and-Tell check-in:* Try to save Show and Tell for the end of group; you need to ask who brought items for Show and Tell and put those individuals on the schedule to share during the large group.
3. *The body's reaction to fear activity:* Discuss the physiological aspects of anxiety during this activity. Similar to other CBT programs (Chansky, 2004; Garland & Clark, 1995), we will use the metaphor of an alarm, stating the following:

An "alarm" goes off in our bodies when there is a real problem—for example, when we are lost, when a large animal confronts us unexpectedly, or when we experience immediate danger such as a house fire. The physical reactions that we feel in these situations are a good thing; the alarm reaction can help us get our bodies ready to handle the situation (i.e., flight or fight). However, some people have overactive, or false, alarms; these are similar to car alarms, smoke alarms, or fire alarms. For example, sometimes a car alarm goes off because another car drives by, not because someone is really breaking into the car. Similarly, fire alarms may go off in school to practice handling a fire, not because there is a real fire. Although the noise is loud, there is no real danger. Having an overactive body alarm can be a problem because our bodies may be tricking us into thinking there is a real danger when, in fact, there is not. When our bodies feel funny or different, we have two jobs. The first job is to calm down so we can think more clearly; the second job is to figure out if the fear is real or false.

- Provide and/or elicit examples of "false alarms" and realistic fears where appropriate. An example of a "false alarm" might include feeling very scared that a small kitten can really hurt you, whereas an example of a real fear may be seeing a burglar in a store. Beware! The children are usually very skilled at identifying isolated examples of danger during this activity, attempting to convince others that there is real danger in events presented as "false alarms" (e.g., bees are *likely* to sting people and the bee-stings are dangerous; or flying on an airplane is unsafe because planes *can* crash). Remind the children of the low probability of those events actually occurring and how it is important not to let worry stand in the way of having fun experiences. Identifying automatic negative thoughts and developing helpful thoughts is discussed in the following session; therefore, the children do not need to completely understand the concept of real versus "false alarms" at this time. Rather, it is more important that they understand that their body reacts to worry and that they can learn to identify their own individual physical reactions to worry. The distinction between real worry and "false alarms" will be reinforced throughout group.
- Pass out the What Worry Does to Your Body worksheet.

  Each group member (parents and group leaders, too) can circle the part of their body that feels funny or different when they worry and/or have a physical reaction to worry. Feel free to add to the picture if your own personal physical experience is missing.

- Help the children identify the chain of physical symptoms and/or signals that tell them they might be having a physical reaction to worry (e.g., a little stomach discomfort, headache, shakiness, feeling warm and flushed in the face).

4. *Facing Your Fears instructional video on relaxation training:* Children and parents will watch a video segment of a therapist working with a 12-year-old boy, teaching the boy the differences between feeling tense and relaxed as well as deep breathing (see accompanying DVD). As the video is introduced, make the connection between the body's response to anxiety and how relaxation and/or deep breathing are tools that can help people calm down and improve emotion regulation. Watch the first portion of the video, then stop the recording and have the children practice what their bodies might feel like when tense and when relaxed. Then watch the second portion of the video and emphasize that deep breathing is one strategy to use when managing both "false alarms" and realistic fears.

Helpful Hint   This is potentially a long time for the large group to be together. If the group has a difficult time being together for this long, you can go over the alarm activity in parent–child dyads and then have the pairs come back together to watch the video.

END—GROUP DIVIDES INTO PARENT–CHILD PAIRS OR TRIOS

On the picture below, circle or color how worry makes *your* body feel. For example, if worrying makes your stomach upset, circle or color the butterflies on the boy's stomach.

What Worry Does to Your Body

▐▐▐▐▐ Parent–Child Pairs or Trios

Materials and/or Worksheets

- Progressive Muscle Relaxation Script worksheet for parents
- Relaxation Practice at Home—Tips! worksheet
- What I Like to Do to Relax worksheet
- Schedule for Calming and/or Relaxing Activities worksheet
- Stress-o-meters
- My Checklist of Fears, Worries, and Irritations worksheet

Goals

1. Parent–child pairs or trios will practice deep breathing as part of relaxation activities.
2. Children will identify two calming activities that they can use throughout the week.
3. Children and parents will identify times throughout the week when they can build in calming activities.
4. Children and parents are introduced to the concept of measuring fear and/or worry and exposure.
5. Children will personalize their stress-o-meters by anchoring them with appropriate descriptors.
6. Children will begin to rate worries using their stress-o-meters.

Activities

1. *Relaxation activity:* This activity directly follows the instructional video of deep breathing. Set up the room with pillows, comfortable chairs, and dim lighting. Introduce the activity by saying the following:

   Deep breathing and other calming activities can help you handle your body's physical reaction to worry. You may want to practice deep breathing at home while watching TV, while riding in the car, or at school—lots of different places. Identifying other calming activities also may be important so that you are doing something every day that may be calming or relaxing. Find the activities that help you the most (see What I Like to Do to Relax worksheet).

- Teach deep breathing, and from now on begin and end each group session with deep breathing exercises. Remember to have the children breathe deeply (belly breathing) and slowly. We will not specifically teach progressive muscle relaxation (PMR) but will provide parents with a worksheet titled Progressive Muscle Relaxation Script. Suggest to parents that they may want to make tapes for their children using the script to encourage relaxation practice at home. In addition, ask parents to read and use the Relaxation Practice At Home—Tips! worksheet to help their children relax at home. Finally, emphasize the importance of positive self-talk (already addressed in the videorecording).

Helpful Hint Make sure that the children are belly breathing (i.e., breathing deeply). Have them put their hands or books on their tummies and move their hands or books by breathing in and out. Make sure that the chairs and environment are as comfortable as possible—use pillows and dim the lighting to set the tone. You may want to pair a positive mantra with the deep breathing—for example, "I can do this," "The worry will go away," and so forth. For children who are extremely resistant to this activity, you can substitute another relaxing activity, such as quietly drawing pictures, or they can look over the worksheets and plan calming activities for home. All of the children

(continued)

should be encouraged to practice these activities at home with their parents. Practice can be paired with positive reinforcement to enhance participation. Keep in mind that not all of the children are likely to respond to all of the strategies or techniques. The purpose of this activity is to introduce the children to a variety of strategies so that they can learn more about and engage in one of them if they so choose. Some of the selected calming activities should be "portable," meaning that the children can use the activities regardless of where they are; emphasize the importance of practicing at home as well as in different settings. An additional purpose is to help enhance the children's self-awareness of physical feelings; at the least, they should be able to contrast physical extremes—for example, "robot" versus "wet noodle."

Helpful Hint Remember that children with neurodevelopmental challenges may not naturally engage in calming or relaxing activities during the day or may use only one or two strategies for calming (e.g., movies, videogames) rather than have a broader repertoire of more portable strategies from which to choose. The purpose of spending so much time on relaxation and alternate activities is to consciously help the children and their parents schedule into their daily routine calming and/or relaxing activities that can be used in multiple environments (including school) so that these activities can happen on a regular basis. Many people engage in calming activities automatically as a way to prevent emotional disregulation as well as to enhance self-regulation when upset, but some children may not naturally engage in these kinds of activities. Throughout group, you can help the families to remember to schedule calming activities into their daily routines until they become a natural and spontaneous part of their day (see Schedule for Calming/Relaxing Activities). As noted above, some of the children may be resistant to trying any of these activities—if so, use a token reward system to increase the likelihood that they try to incorporate some of these activities into their daily routines.

2. *What I Like to Do to Relax worksheet:* Remind the group of the connection between the body's physical response to worry and the importance of engaging in calming and/or relaxing activities.

    We all need to control our body's reaction to anxiety or stress so that we can think and make a plan. We can calm our bodies in different ways—deep breathing, relaxation, exercise, humor, and/ or listening to music as well as any other activities you find to be helpful.

    • The What I Like to Do to Relax worksheet lists suggestions for individualized calming activities—taking a bath, reading a book, doing an art project, finding the right surface to sit on (e.g., bean bag, lumpy couch, straight-back chair), and so forth. Each child should identify activities that he or she finds calming (during group if there is time; if not, at home), and complete the worksheet. Then, each child may complete the accompanying Schedule for Calming and/or Relaxing Activities worksheet, designating times during the week when they plan to engage in calming activities. Again, each child will likely find different activities calming.

3. *Stress-o-meters:* Introduce the idea of measuring fear/worry—and how these feelings go up and down.

    What goes up, must come down; anxious feelings go up but they always come down.

    In this session, the children will receive their own stress-o-meters (or if there is time in group, you can have precut materials and have the children assemble their own; see pictures of stress-o-meters).

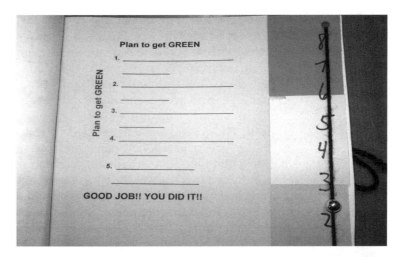

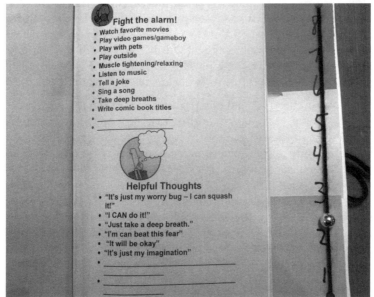

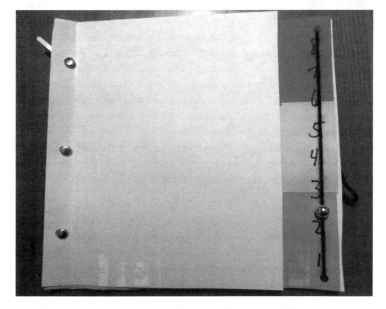

Examples of stress-o-meters. Note that red is on top, yellow is in the middle, and green is on the bottom.

For this project you will need the following materials: Two sheets of thick construction paper for the front and back cover (dimensions: 1 sheet = 8 ½ inches x 6 ½ inches; second piece = 8 ½ inches x 8 ½ inches); sheets of red, green, and yellow construction paper; glue sticks; hole puncher; yarn or string; scissors; brads, or other fasteners; markers and small beads. The pages within the stress-o-meter should be already prepared and ready to be included in the stress-o-meter. The inside pages should include a page for the child's name, a page for strategies the child can use when anxious or upset (see example, with headings of "Fight the Alarm!" and Helpful Thoughts") and a page titled "Plan to Get to Green."

To get started, cut strips of red, green, and yellow paper and glue on the back cover page (larger of the two thick construction pieces; see example). Write numbers along the right-hand side of the page from 1–8. Punch two holes in the back cover; along the right-hand side, thread the yarn or string in the holes along with one small bead and secure by tying a knot in the back of the cover. Sequence front cover (smaller piece of construction paper), inner pages, and back cover together and punch three holes along the left side of the materials. Insert a brad or other fastener in the holes.

Now the children will need to personalize the stress-o-meters. They will begin by anchoring the rating scale with descriptive words for their level of anxiety. They can start with extremes (1, 8) and then fill in the middles ranges. If the children get stuck thinking of words to use, their parents can suggest words that may describe their child's overt behavior (behavioral anchors) such as crying, screaming, pacing (8) versus talking calmly, sitting down, listening to others (1).

- Each stress-o-meter has a list of suggestions that the children can choose from to be part of their plan to decrease worry and/or fear. Not all of the pages contain content that has been reviewed already (e.g., helpful thoughts, facing fears a little at a time). The primary purpose of introducing the stress-o-meter at this point is to begin to help the children and their parents measure anxiety. The remaining concepts will be addressed in subsequent sessions.

  The stress-o-meters also can be used to develop a plan for getting to and staying in the green zone. Specific strategies for helping the children "get to green," especially when in the red zones, will be discussed in the parent group in Session 5. Specific suggestions include the following:

  — Handle your body's reactions (e.g., deep breathing, taking a walk, reading a book).
  — Think helpful thoughts (e.g., "Fight back with facts"; "It's just my worry bug again"; "I can beat this"; "I can't think clearly when I am upset, I need to calm myself down"; "I can do something else while I am waiting for my worry and/or anxiety to go away"; task-neutral thoughts that help the children focus on the task or activity at hand—for example, when giving a book report in class, thinking, "I know the material—I just need to read the report so that others can learn from my information" [introduced more completely in Session 5]).
  — Think about advice from friends. This will include selected suggestions from the ongoing advice list that the group has worked on and created since the first group session.
  — Face fear a little at a time: Introduce the concept of exposure. Tell children and parents that the best way to get over fears and worries is to face them a little at a time. This concept, too, is introduced more completely in Session 5.

4. *Share time:* Encourage group members to share any of the worksheets or the stress-o-meter.
5. *Worry checklist:* The My Checklist of Fears, Worries, and Irritations worksheet will be used to help children practice using their rating scales. Parents and children together can go down the list, pick a few worries, and then state what rating on their stress-o-meter they

would give themselves if faced with that situation or when they think about themselves in that situation. These ratings can be used to help children and parents identify the worries or anxieties that the children will be facing first.

Helpful Hint The children likely will struggle with measuring anxiety. To help them become more accurate in their stress-o-meter ratings, they will need lots of practice matching their ratings with those of an observer—either a parent or therapist. Initially, parents or other adults may need to provide the anxiety ratings rather than asking the children to generate their own ratings (e.g., "You look like you might be at a 6"). The children may disagree with the adult's ratings and/or may respond quite negatively to feedback from their parents. It will be important to balance giving feedback to the children about their behavior with recognizing that the feedback may actually exacerbate the situation. Working with children when they are in the "red zone" will be discussed in more detail during the parent group of Session 5.

Helpful Hint Our experience has been that the children and parent ratings can be quite discrepant. As with previous activities, you do not need to push agreement but rather discuss the differences. Strategies for supporting calm behavior may include teaching parents to reinforce their children's behavior when they are in the "green zone" by stating something such as, "You look calm and relaxed right now; good job staying in green." Tangible reinforcers also may be used to help children stay in the "green zone." Eventually, the parents can use the stress-o-meter to encourage coping strategies when their child is in the "yellow zone" or "red zone." The children also can be encouraged to use the stress-o-meter when they are approaching anxious situations at home or in group and to watch anxiety decrease as they handle the tasks. The stress-o-meters will become particularly important and useful as the children are introduced to the concept of graded exposure in Sessions 5 and 6.

END—GO BACK TO LARGE GROUP

Progressive Muscle Relaxation Script

The following is a script you can use when working with your child to help him or her relax. Note: Before beginning the relaxation exercise, isolate and practice with your child each of the following muscle movements: 1) squeeze arms and hands tightly; 2) squeeze legs tightly, toes flat; 3) tense face muscles; 4) squeeze stomach muscles; and 5) tense the whole body. Then, have your child identify a special calming place that you can describe when you get to the "visualization" portion of the script.

GETTING COMFORTABLE (At this point, the parent begins to read the script to the child.)

Go ahead and settle back so you feel comfortable. Let all of your muscles go loose and heavy. Close your eyes and take three deep, slow breaths. As you breathe in slowly, concentrate on the air as it fills your lungs; and as you breathe out slowly, notice your breath rushing out through your nose and mouth. Breathe slowly, thinking about the feeling of air passing in (pause) and out of your body (pause).

Arms and Hands

Now, pretend you have a whole lemon in each of your hands. Squeeze the lemons as hard as you can—try to squeeze all of the juice out. While you're squeezing both hands, make a muscle with your upper arms as well so that your arms and hands are tight and squeezed. Hold that tight feeling in your arms as I begin to count.... 5...4...3...2...1.... Now, drop the lemon and relax your fist and arm. Notice the feelings of warmth and relaxation that flow through your fingers into your hands and arms. Now, squeeze those lemons again as hard as you can. Feel the muscles in your hands, lower arms, and upper arms tighten and squeeze. Hold that tight feeling in your arms as I count.... 5...4...3...2...1...relax. Notice how the tight feeling leaves your arms and is replaced by the warm, heavy feelings of relaxation (pause).

Legs

Now, squeeze your legs as tight as you can, make a muscle in your upper leg and lower leg, and curl your toes as tight as you can so that your whole legs on both sides are tight and squeezed. Hold that tightness while I count.... 5...4...3...2...1.... Let the tightness in your legs go loose (pause). Do it again.

(continued)

(continued)

Progressive Muscle Relaxation Script

Face

Now I want you to scrunch up your face like you just bit into something really sour, like a lemon. Wrinkle up your forehead, your nose, your mouth, and your cheeks; squeeze your eyes shut as tight as you can.... 5...4...3...2...1.... Now, relax (pause); smooth out all the wrinkles in your forehead, nose, mouth, cheeks, and eyes.... Breathe deeply as you notice the warm, heavy feelings of relaxation in your body. Do it again.

Stomach

Now, pretend you're lying on your back and an elephant is about to step on your stomach. Tighten up your stomach muscles harder and harder, and pay attention to your stomach muscles as I count down.... 5...4...3...2...1.... Relax your stomach muscles and feel how warm, heavy, and relaxed your stomach feels.

Whole Body

Now, I want you to tighten your whole body, from your scrunched up face to your hunched shoulders, your tight fists and arms, your stiff back and stomach, and your tight legs and curled toes. Make your whole body stiff as a board and hold it as I count.... 5...4...3...2...1.... Let go and relax (pause). Just relax and feel how warm and heavy your whole body feels. Relax.

Visualization

With your eyes closed, I want you to imagine that you're in a forest.... (Describe the place; focus on the sensory details such as the warmth or coolness of the air, the soft sounds in the background, the sunlight on your face, the smell of the earth and pine trees.) Now it's time to leave your special place and come back to this room. We're going to take five imaginary steps, each step moving farther away from the forest and closer to this room. I'll count each step out for you. 5...You're stepping away from your special place.... 4...You've moved a little farther away from the forest.... 3...You're half way back to this room.... 2...You're almost here, just one small step away.... 1...And you're back. When you feel ready, go ahead and open your eyes.

Relaxation Practice at Home—Tips!

The practice of relaxation is one of the most basic anxiety-reducing techniques. For some children, physical relaxation (e.g., deep breathing) works best for calming; for others, relaxing the mind is most helpful. Whatever strategy your child chooses as his preferred approach, he will need to practice. Sound easy? In theory, it is. However, the ability to relax in daily life requires learning and practice. Below you will find three common approaches to relaxation that you can practice at home with your child. Which one works best for him? Which one does he like doing?

 Deep breathing: Have your child sit up in a chair in a comfortable position wearing loose clothing. Encourage her to breathe in slowly to a count of 5; then, slowly exhale, making sure that the exhale is longer than the inhale. After your child has practiced a few times, have your child place her hand on her stomach and ask your child to make her stomach move out as she breathes in deeply (e.g., "Blow up your tummy like a beach ball"). Repeat the inhalation, hold breath, and exhalation sequence a number of times. Sometimes, children like to practice deep breathing right before they go to sleep.

 Body mindfulness: Have your child practice experiencing the difference between being tense and tight and relaxed and loose. Pretend to be a robot. Walk around the room with stiff legs, arms, and body. Talk about what it feels like. Then, flop down in a chair like a wet noodle. Talk about what it feels like in your body to be floppy and droopy like a wet noodle. During the day, if you notice that your child is stiff and tense, remind him about the robot and wet noodle. How can he get his body to be more relaxed like a wet noodle? Learning to distinguish between a relaxed and a tense state is an important skill for your child to develop.

 Using self-talk: Positive self-talk can be helpful for some children. Brainstorm with your child about some helpful sayings that might work for her (e.g., "I can beat my worries," "Just breathe, I can do it!"). When your child has selected a saying, have her practice with deep breathing. For other children, particularly children with intense special interests or preoccupations, (e.g., animals, movies, video games), it may be calming to think about their favorite interests as a way to calm down. For example, listing favorite animals or characters may be a useful strategy for some children when upset.

 Remember, the goal of relaxation is to bring your baseline level of arousal down to a lower level. All of these coping techniques work best when anxiety is not yet severe. Try them out during everyday activities, such as when your child just wakes up in the morning, before he heads off to school, or when he is beginning to become a little overaroused.

GOOD LUCK TRYING THESE OUT! WE LOOK FORWARD TO HEARING HOW IT GOES.

We just practiced deep breathing to help our body's reaction to worry. Using the list on the next page as a guideline, think about what else you can do to help your body relax. How can you help your body feel better so you can think and make a plan to handle your worry?

What do you like to do to relax?

Circle your favorite activities on the following page.

If your favorite activities are not on the list, write them down! Figure out when you'll do these activities, and write them in on the Schedule for Calming and/or Relaxing Activities worksheet.

Post these pages in your house so that you can remember to relax every day!

What does worry do to your body?

What I Like to Do to Relax

Listen to music	Play my musical instrument
Play with my pet	Take a warm bath
Read a book	Snuggle up with pillows
Go for a walk	Sit quietly
Jump on the trampoline	Sing
Play a sport	Cook
Ride a bike	Draw pictures
Watch television	Talk with a friend
Play video games	Write in a journal
Play with and/or collect trading cards	Squeeze a Koosh ball

What else?

_____

_____

_____

_____

Schedule for Calming and/or Relaxing Activities

Calming Activities	Sunday	Monday	Tuesday	Wednesday	Thursday	Friday	Saturday
1.							
2.							
3.							
4.							
5.							
6.							
7.							
8.							

Reward Plan:

Completing 1–2 activities per week = _____

Completing 3–4 activities per week = _____

Completing 5–6+ activities per week = _____

On the next page, look at the list of worries and fears with your mom or dad.

Which ones do you worry about sometimes?
Which ones do you worry about a lot?
Which ones do you never worry about?

Most important, select the fears or worries that get in your way. If you want to, you can add other fears and/or worries in the blanks on your checklist.

Next, think about where you would be on your stress-o-meter if faced with one of your worry situations. Write the number next to the worry.

My Checklist of Fears, Worries, and Irritations

I'm afraid of, worried about, or irritated about . . .

	No	Sometimes	A lot	Stress-o-meter rating (1–8)
Being late				
Being home alone				
Making mistakes				
The dark				
Letting go of past events				
Dogs and/or cats				
Storms and/or tornados				
Bugs, spiders, and/or bees				
Getting a disease				
Being teased				
Germs				
Trying new foods				
Being away from family				
Using public bathrooms				
Talking to new people				
Talking in school				
Getting to sleep				
Scary movies				
Changes				
Asking for help				
Parents going out				
Getting lost				
Dying				
Starting homework				
World events				
Going to someone's house				
Loud noises				
Heights				
Starting a conversation				
Being in a room by myself				
Performing in front of others				
Other:				

⁞⁞⁞⁞⁞ Large Group

Materials and/or Worksheets

- Props for Show and Tell

Goals

1. Children will share Show and Tell, emphasizing that when they spend less time worrying they can spend more time doing the activities they enjoy.

Activities

1. *Show and Tell:* Follow up here with any of the children who want to participate. Remember, Show and Tell can also be a good opportunity to practice social skills (e.g., asking questions, giving compliments, presenting in front of a group).
2. *Deep breathing:* Because this strategy was introduced earlier in this session, it will now become part of an opening and closing ritual. Children can take turns leading the deep breathing exercise.

Assignments

1. Complete any unfinished worksheets.
2. Bring Show and Tell next week if they did not present today.
3. Review when children are going to engage in relaxing activities.
4. *Closing/good-bye:* Continue with advice poster, and give children prizes for sticker cards.

END SESSION 4

Session Notes

_____

_____

_____

_____

_____

_____

_____

_____

_____

Session Notes

_____

_____

_____

_____

_____

_____

_____

_____

_____

_____

_____

_____

_____

_____

_____

_____

_____

_____

_____

_____

_____

_____

_____

_____

_____

_____

_____

The Mind–Body Connection

The purpose of Session 5 is to continue to emphasize the physiological impact of anxiety and how it can influence thoughts or cognitions. A review of deep breathing and/or other calming activities also occurs in this session. The connection between thoughts, feelings, and the body's physical reactions to anxiety is introduced. In addition, the session teaches about the connection between parenting behaviors, parenting a child with neurodevelopmental challenges, and supporting children in facing fears. The parents also receive instruction about how to support their children when they are in the "red zone" (the zone on the stress-o-meter that indicates an individual is feeling highly anxious or upset). In addition, parents learn the differences between realistic and unrealistic fears and the subsequent implications for treatment.

SESSION STRUCTURE

- Large group, children and parents together
- Parent–child pairs or trios
- Parent group and child group breakout sessions (occur simultaneously)
- Large group, children and parents together

SAMPLE SCHEDULE: THE MIND–BODY CONNECTION

- **Large Group** (15–20 minutes)
    - Snack
    - Discussion: Review of schedule and check-in with Show and Tell
    - Deep breathing

- **Parent–Child Pairs or Trios** (35 minutes)
    - Calming and/or relaxing activity schedule
    - Finish stress-o-meters and rating worry
    - Finding My Target worksheet—where to begin
    - Tracking worries and/or fears
    - Share time

- **Child Group** (25 minutes)
    - Active Minds worksheets
    - Helpful Thoughts worksheets
    - Storytime

- **Parent Group** (25 minutes)

- **Large Group** (10–15 minutes)
  - Show and Tell
  - Deep breathing
  - Prizes

SOCIAL SKILLS

- Greeting others by name
- Sharing personal information in front of a group
- Working cooperatively as part of a group (Active Minds and Helpful Thoughts worksheets activity)
- Listening to others
- Asking questions and making comments during Show and Tell

Suggestions for Supporting Social Skills

- Encourage effort and any approximation toward participation, but do not force.
- Provide verbal and/or visual support (use worksheets). These can be provided by parents and facilitators.
- Model social skills.
- Use rewards for participation.

▥▥▥▥ Large Group (Children and Parents Together)

Materials and/or Worksheets

- Snacks
- Written schedule
- Written list of rules, posted on the wall if necessary
- Pencils and/or markers

Goals

1. Children will describe one or two times that they either practiced relaxation techniques or engaged in a calming and/or relaxing activity.
2. Children will practice deep breathing.

Activities

1. *Snack:* Provide a variety of drinks and snack foods for parents and children when they arrive for group.
2. *Discussion*

   - Review with families the calming activities and strategies from the previous session and whether families had a chance to engage in these activities during the week. Ask them to talk about what other relaxing and/or calming activities they preferred to engage in over the course of the week. If children are not able to identify any activities, you and the parents may provide examples of what you did to relax or calm down during the week as a means of modeling sharing in the group. Remember, these are skills you are teaching; therefore, it may take a few sessions or longer for these activities to occur regularly during the course of the week.

- If some of the children did not get to present Show and Tell last session, make sure it is part of the schedule for today.
- Introduce the main theme for the day—learning how "false alarms" can trick one into false beliefs or "active minds."

3. *Deep breathing:* Children and parents will practice deep breathing, taking three to four deep breaths.

END—GROUP DIVIDES INTO PARENT–CHILD PAIRS OR TRIOS

▐▐▐▐▐ Parent–Child Pairs or Trios

Materials and/or Worksheets

- What I Like to Do to Relax worksheet (from Session 4); complete if necessary
- My Checklist of Fears, Worries, and Irritations worksheet (from Session 4); complete if necessary
- Steps to Success: Finding My Target worksheet
- Fear Tracker worksheet

Goals

1. Children and parents will complete calming activities schedule if not completed from last week.
2. Children will complete personalization of their stress-o-meters by anchoring them with appropriate descriptors.
3. Children will rate worries using their stress-o-meters (from Session 4).
4. Children will select worries and/or fears to work on and put them on the Finding My Target worksheet.

Activities

Calming and/or relaxing activities: Remind the group of the connection between the body's physical reaction to worry and relaxing activities. Tell the participants:

Relaxation, deep breathing, and other calming activities are tools you can use to get your physical feelings or reactions under control, regardless of whether your body is reacting to a real danger or a "false alarm."

1. Complete the What I Like to Do to Relax worksheet if necessary.
2. *Stress-o-meters:* Complete the stress-o-meters (see Session 4).
3. *Worry checklist (continued from last week):* The worksheet My Checklist of Fears, Worries, and Irritations will be used to help children practice using their rating scales. Parents and children together can go down the list, pick a few worries, and then state where they would be on their stress-o-meter if faced with that situation. Remember to pick situations that interfere with the child's day-to-day functioning. For example, people can be frightened of or worry about tornados, but there may be no evidence on a daily basis of this fear interfering with a person's daily life. However, if a child cannot go outside on cloudy days and refuses to sit near windows when it rains, then fear of tornados may be a good fear to target. This process of rating worries is important because the worries that are identified and rated here will be the same worries or anxieties that the children will tackle first (see Steps to Success: Finding My Target worksheet on the next page).

4. *Finding My Target worksheet:* Children and parents will use the Steps to Success: Finding My Target worksheet to help identify the worries and fears that a child will begin to face over the course of the group treatment. This worksheet helps children rank their worries from those that are "not much of a worry" to those that are the "biggest worry." These designations are intended to help children and their parents sort through the list of worries and select five or so priority worries or fears. The priority worries typically are the worries that cause the greatest amount of interference in the child's life *and* that the child wants to address first (ratings of greater than 4 on the stress-o-meter may be a good indicator of interference); however, children also may select worries that are "medium" or "pretty big" as priority fears so that they may experience some success facing fears. Fears that are considered a "bit of a worry" and/or "not much of a worry" typically will not be considered priority worries.

5. *Fear Tracker worksheet:* For this session, write the priority worries on the Fear Tracker worksheet along with parent and child ratings of each worry. For each session from this point forward, we will ask parents and children at the beginning of each session to rate these fears again on a scale from 1 to 8.

6. *Share time:* Discuss the five fears each child will be tracking on their Fear Tracker. Look for similarities between the children's selected fears and highlight those similarities as the fears are discussed.

7. It is important that the parent–child pairs of trios understand this activity as much as possible, because if they do not finish the worksheets in group, it will be necessary for them to finish the activities at home so they are ready to go with their Fear Tracker worksheets next session.

Helpful Hint   The purpose of the Fear Tracker worksheet is to monitor the top fears and/or worries that the children have identified for themselves on a weekly basis even though the fears may not yet have been addressed directly. This activity is intended to go quickly, with parents and children rating the intensity and/or interference of their fears and/or worries without much discussion. It is not important for the parents and children to agree, but it may be helpful for them to briefly understand their differences.

END—GROUP DIVIDES INTO PARENT GROUP AND CHILD GROUP

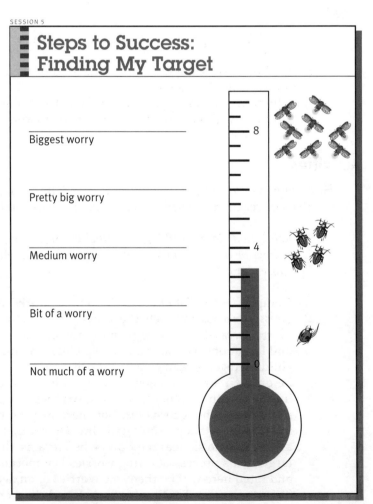

SESSION 5

Steps to Success: Finding My Target

Biggest worry

8

Pretty big worry

Medium worry

4

Bit of a worry

Not much of a worry

0

Fear Tracker

Identify up to five fears and/or worries that get in your way. Using your stress-o-meter, please rate on a scale of 1–8 (with 1 meaning *not much of a worry* and 8 meaning *the biggest worry*) the level of stress and/or anxiety you experience when faced with each fear.

Fears	Week 5		Week 6		Week 7		Week 8		Week 9		Week 10	
	Parent	Child	Parent	Child	Parent	Child	Parent	Child	Parent	Child	Parent	Child
1.												
2.												
3.												
4.												
5.												

Fears	Week 11		Week 12		Week 13		Week 14		Booster session	
	Parent	Child	Parent	Child	Parent	Child	Parent	Child	Parent	Child
1.										
2.										
3.										
4.										
5.										

‖‖‖‖‖ Child Group

Materials and/or Worksheets

- Set of Active Minds and Helpful Thoughts worksheets
- Suggestions for Helpful Thoughts worksheet
- *Parts* (Arnold, 1997)

Goals

1. Children will identify between three and five examples of negative thoughts in the Active Minds: At the Zoo One Day… worksheet.
2. Children will identify between three and five helpful thoughts for the boy at the zoo.
3. Children will generate three negative thoughts when presented with their own fear.
4. Children will generate two helpful thoughts for a peer's fear.
5. Children will generate helpful thoughts for their own fears and/or worries.

Activities

1. *Active Minds activity:* Go over the Active Minds: At the Zoo One Day… worksheet. Have the children write down (either individually or as a group—see below) how they think the boy's thoughts might make his body feel. Emphasize the following:

   Uncomfortable physical feelings can make our minds active (Garland & Clark, 1995). Active minds make it hard to tell whether a fear is a real danger or a "false alarm."

   - For this boy and his fear of snakes, label the fears expressed in the bubbles above the boy's head as either "false alarms" or real dangers (where appropriate). This activity works best as a group problem-solving activity, especially for younger children. You can create a picture of a stick figure on a large sheet of paper and draw thought bubbles for the figure. The children can take turns completing the large worksheet together by filling in the thought bubbles one at a time as they generate both imaginings of "active minds" and "helpful thoughts." They can even come up with a different fearful situation to-gether (e.g., facing fears of spiders or bees). They can use their individual worksheets as a guide or to write down the group's answers if they wish. Make the connection between active minds—minds that overreact to a certain situation—and the body's reaction to worry. You can have the children determine where they think the boy would rate himself on a stress-o-meter; alternatively, you can have the children rate whether the boy is in a red, yellow, or green zone as he thinks about snakes.
   - Once the children have identified whether the boy's fears are real or "false alarms," have them complete the Helpful Thoughts: At the Zoo One Day…worksheet to generate other things the boy could say to himself to help his body feel less anxious. Encourage the group to fight back with facts; that is, to generate facts as a way to beat the anxiety. Ask the children where they think the boy's fear rates on his stress-o-meter once he has used "helpful thoughts." What color zone (red, yellow, or green) does his anxiety level fall in?
   - Next, ask the children to complete their own Active Minds worksheets. Have them write down their own fears and add negative thoughts in the thought bubbles. At the bottom of the sheet, ask the children to circle how their bodies feel when they think negative thoughts.

- Children will then complete the Helpful Thoughts worksheet with empty thought bubbles for the identified problem situation. If the children need assistance, they can first pass these sheets to a friend and ask him or her to generate at least two suggestions for helpful thoughts. Then the child can finish the worksheet on his or her own. Ask the children to circle at the bottom of the worksheet how their bodies will feel when they are thinking helpful thoughts. The children also may want to use the Suggestions for Helpful Thoughts worksheet if they are having trouble generating ideas.
- Ask the children to complete an entire set of Active Minds and Helpful Thoughts worksheets on their own at home.

2. *Storytime:* Read the book *Parts* (Arnold, 1997) to the children because it is a good example of negative thinking and the mind–body connection. As you read the book, you can pause at various points in the book to highlight "active minds" and "false alarms." For example, when the character in the book talks about going bald or "losing his mind," ask the children,

   Is this a real danger or a "false alarm"?

   - After the book is over, ask the children to identify the character's specific thoughts that made him feel worse and what he could have thought instead to help himself feel better. Feel free to write the answers on a poster board. As with other storytimes, feel free to eliminate this activity if the books are seen as too young for the group.

END—BACK TO LARGE GROUP

On the next page, you will meet Matthew, who is afraid of snakes. When he goes to the zoo and sees a snake, his mind becomes very active, he begins to think a lot about the snake, and he worries about what might happen.

How will Matthew's body feel when he thinks these thoughts?

Take a look and see!

What do you think?

Active Minds

At the zoo one day . . .

I can't look at the snake! It's so scary!

Uh oh. It's going to get out of its cage.

I have to get out of here!

What if it escapes and comes to my house?

I'm never going to the zoo again!

It's going to kill me! Oh no, maybe it will kill my mom!

What if there are snakes in my backyard? I can't play ball!

A snake in a cage at the Snake House

Will thinking these thoughts make him feel better or worse?

On the next page, see if you can help Matthew. Write down what the boy might think or say to help his body feel less anxious when he sees the snake.

How will Matthew's body feel when he thinks these thoughts?

What do you think?

Suggestions for Helpful Thoughts

"This is just a 'false alarm.'"

"I can face my fear; nothing bad will happen."

"The worry feelings will go away."

"I can handle this."

"This is no big deal."

"It's my worry bug; I can squash it!"

"I can fight back with facts."

> Fight back with facts:
>
> The glass cage is very thick.
>
> Snakes hardly ever escape from cages.
>
> The snake does not know where I live.

▐▐▐▐▐ Parent Group

Materials and/or Worksheets

- Set of Active Minds and Helpful Thoughts worksheets
- Plan to Get to Green worksheet
- Cycle of Anxiety worksheet
- Anxiety Components: A Fearful Experience at the Zoo worksheet
- Parental Protection worksheet
- Anxiety/Exposure graph
- Frank's Fears worksheets
- My Child's Realistic and Unrealistic ("False Alarm") Fears worksheet

Goals

1. Parents will be introduced to the Active Minds and Helpful Thoughts worksheets.
2. Parents will create a plan for getting to "green" (i.e., green zone on the stress-o-meter) when their children are in "red" (i.e., red zone on the stress-o-meter).
3. Parents will be introduced to the Cycle of Anxiety worksheet and will learn about the connection between parenting style and their child's behavior.
4. Parents will be introduced to the concepts of adaptive protection and excessive protection.
5. Parents will be introduced to and eventually be able to identify realistic and/or unrealistic fears in their children.

Activities

1. Briefly review the Active Minds and Helpful Thoughts worksheets so that the parents have an idea of what their children are working on in group. The children will be completing their own worksheets at home for an assignment; therefore, make sure parents know this and can help their children.
2. Develop a plan for when children are in the "red" zone. Talk with the parents about the following steps:

   - Create a plan for getting to "green." Here, the child and parent together select strategies that the child can use to help him or her go from red to yellow and from yellow to green. Some of these strategies might include deep breathing, taking a break, or moving away from a situation. Be as specific as possible. Emphasize the importance of moving one step at a time (i.e., from a stress-o-meter rating of 8 to 7, then 7 to 6, and so forth). It is also helpful to establish with the child whether he or she prefers to have his or her parent present when upset or if he or she can tolerate the parent going to another room.
   - Establish a reward system so that the child is rewarded for using appropriate strategies to help calm down.
   - Many children might be reactive to any verbal direction when they are in the "red" zone. In these situations, the parents are encouraged to work only toward helping the children calm down. Parents may need to be coached *not* to try to problem-solve the situation, *not* to ask questions, and *not* to provide verbal reminders to their child such as "just calm down" or "take deep breaths." Rather, parents can take deep breaths themselves and say out loud what they are doing to calm down themselves (e.g., "I am going to take a break," "I am going to go to my room for a few minutes and relax").
   - For children who can become agitated quite quickly, it is important to establish a reward program for staying in "green" and again for implementing strategies that help her move from red to yellow and yellow to green. See the Plan to Get Green worksheet.

3. Introduce the idea of how parental anxiety can influence child anxiety. The worksheet Cycle of Anxiety can be introduced here. Tell parents the following:

    Anxiety can lead to an increased perception of danger in the environment, which can lead to avoidance. Avoidance, in turn, leads to a lack of opportunity to develop coping strategies, which leads to increased anxiety, which then leads to an increased perception of danger in the environment.

4. The Anxiety Components worksheet helps illustrate how the *perception* of specific situations can lead to fearful and avoidant behavior. For example, some people may *view* the situation at the zoo as worrisome because of a fear of snakes; avoidant behavior results from this faulty perception, which leads to continued anxious feelings and more avoidance.

5. Introduce the concepts of *adaptive protection* and *excessive protection*.

    Adaptive protection is a functional parental response that may occur when children have marked areas of developmental, physical, or emotional challenge. Children with extensive challenges may experience "realistic" fears in their everyday lives; as a result, parents and other caregivers must carefully limit their children's exposure to challenging environmental events to create multiple success experiences for them over time. Excessive protection, however, is a parenting style that limits a child's exposure to anxiety-provoking situations through avoidant behavior, thus reducing the number of opportunities children may have to generate and practice effective coping strategies for handling these situations.

6. Encourage parents to explore these concepts through the Parental Protection worksheet.

7. The Anxiety/Exposure Graph visually displays the fact that individuals can habituate or get used to worry and/or anxiety over time. When an individual is in a stressful situation and then leaves, anxiety drops quickly. This can teach individuals that fleeing an anxiety-producing situation is the fastest way to reduce anxious feelings. Remaining in the anxiety-producing situation may seem counterintuitive. However, staying in the anxious situation over time is truly the most effective way to handle anxiety; by remaining in the situation long enough, children will gain the awareness and experience that anxious feelings can become less intense over time. Children need the opportunity to get used to anxious feelings and see that they can be manageable.

8. To help parents concretize these concepts, they will complete a series of worksheets—Frank's Fears—that help them sort realistic fears from those that are unrealistic ("false alarms"). Begin with a hypothetical scenario of a child named Frank who has several realistic and unrealistic fears. You may say,

    All fears have some element of reality to them, but the likelihood of some of these events happening is very slim.

9. This may help parents as they sort through realistic and unrealistic fear situations for their children. This activity is particularly important because determining whether a fear is realistic or unrealistic will determine treatment direction. For example, anxious feelings when going to math may be because of a math disability (realistic fear), which might point to the need for additional math support. Conversely, anxious feelings when riding the school bus because of a fear of getting into an accident (unrealistic fear) may warrant a different approach. Once the parents have worked through the Frank's Fears worksheets, have them complete the My Child's Realistic and Unrealistic ("False Alarm") Fears worksheet. This may be done during group or, if time is short, finished at home.

Helpful Hint   This is clearly a lot of information to cover. However, it is helpful to review the concepts of *adaptive* and *excessive protection*, the "cycle of anxiety," and unrealistic and realistic fears all at the same time, at least briefly. You can then use a hypothetical scenario—the Frank's Fears worksheets—to help parents sort fears into "realistic" and "unrealistic" categories together as a group before asking parents to sort their own child's fears into categories. Because these are such critical concepts, you will need to continue to review them over the next few sessions.

END—BACK TO LARGE GROUP

Now it's your turn! Think about a situation that makes you feel really anxious or worried. For example, maybe you feel really anxious when you hear thunder.

On the next page, write down the situation in the space at the top of the worksheet.

Next, think about how your body feels and what happens when your mind becomes active. What does your ACTIVE MIND say? What are you thinking during this situation? Will thinking these thoughts make your body feel better or worse?

Write down how your body feels and what your thoughts are in the thought bubbles.

Now, think of some helpful thoughts that would make you feel better in this situation.

How will your body feel if you think helpful thoughts?

Write your helpful thoughts down on the next page!

Plan to Get to Green

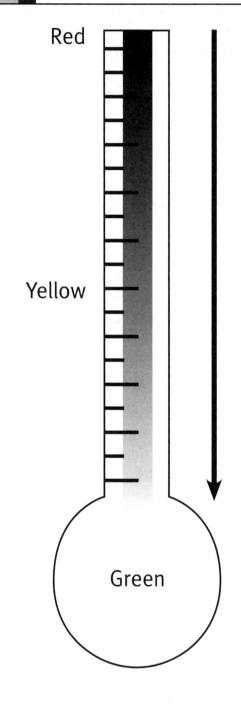

Red

Yellow

Green

Helpful Hints

What helps the most
when my child is in red?

What makes things worse?

Managing active minds ("false alarm"):

Helpful thoughts

Fight fears with facts

_____

Managing the body's reaction:

Deep breathing

_____

_____

Rewards for moving from red to yellow
and from yellow to green:

_____

_____

Rewards for staying in green:

_____

_____

Cycle of Anxiety

We will be reviewing the cycle of anxiety today. The handout **Anxiety Components: A Fearful Experience at the Zoo** illustrates how the body's physical reactions to a feared situation lead to increased thoughts of danger, which then lead to avoidance of the fearful situation. This cycle of behavior ultimately results in fewer opportunities to practice coping skills and increases perceptions of danger. Your child will be introduced to this concept through the story of Matthew. We'll use the example of Matthew's trip to the zoo to illustrate the cycle of anxiety.

We will then discuss the concepts of adaptive and excessive protection. *Adaptive protection* is a functional parenting style that may occur when children have marked areas of developmental, physical, or emotional challenges. For example, children with extensive challenges may experience "realistic" fears in their everyday lives, and as a result, parents must carefully limit their children's exposure to challenging events to create multiple success experiences for them over time. Excessive protection, however, is a parenting style that may limit the child's exposure to anxiety-producing situations even though the child may possess the necessary developmental skills to be successful in the situation. The parent's efforts are directed at unnecessarily protecting the child from fearful situations by avoiding the situation altogether. As a result, the child may not learn the coping skills necessary to later face this situation.

The **Anxiety/Exposure Graph** visually displays the fact that individuals can habituate or get used to worry and/or anxiety over time. When an individual is in a stressful situation and then leaves, anxiety drops quickly. This can teach individuals that fleeing an anxiety-producing situation is the fastest way to reduce anxious feelings. Remaining in the anxiety-producing situation may seem counterintuitive. However, staying in the anxious situation over time is truly the most effective way to handle anxiety; by remaining in the situation long enough, children will gain the awareness and experience that anxious feelings can become less intense over time. Children need the opportunity to get used to anxious feelings and see that they can be manageable.

We will then discuss the difference between realistic and unrealistic fears by completing a series of worksheets about a boy named Frank **(Frank's Fears)**. The difference between realistic fear and unrealistic fear (i.e., "false alarms") is important, because this distinction will guide you in the strategies you select to help your child. The handouts on Frank's fears illustrate the different intervention strategies you may use. Remember, even if your child is facing a realistic fear, using strategies to calm the body (e.g., deep breathing) can still help.

We would then like you to distinguish between your child's realistic and unrealistic fears. We will review this worksheet **(My Child's Realistic and Unrealistic ["False Alarm"] Fears)** again next week.

Anxiety Components
A Fearful Experience at the Zoo

Fewer opportunities to practice facing fears

Decreased learning and coping

Physical reactions

Heart racing, sweating, butterflies in stomach as you approach the snake cage

Behaviors

Thoughts

Avoid the snake cage and/or the zoo

The snake might get out of its cage!

Parental Protection
The Interaction Between Your Parenting and Your Child's Ability

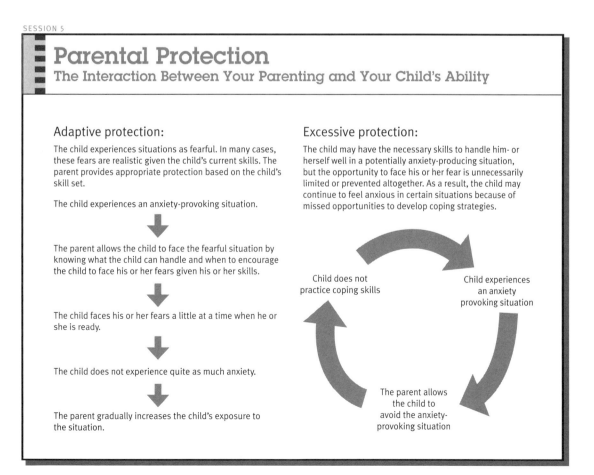

Adaptive protection:

The child experiences situations as fearful. In many cases, these fears are realistic given the child's current skills. The parent provides appropriate protection based on the child's skill set.

The child experiences an anxiety-provoking situation.

The parent allows the child to face the fearful situation by knowing what the child can handle and when to encourage the child to face his or her fears given his or her skills.

The child faces his or her fears a little at a time when he or she is ready.

The child does not experience quite as much anxiety.

The parent gradually increases the child's exposure to the situation.

Excessive protection:

The child may have the necessary skills to handle him- or herself well in a potentially anxiety-producing situation, but the opportunity to face his or her fear is unnecessarily limited or prevented altogether. As a result, the child may continue to feel anxious in certain situations because of missed opportunities to develop coping strategies.

Child does not practice coping skills

Child experiences an anxiety provoking situation

The parent allows the child to avoid the anxiety-provoking situation

Graph of Anxiety Level Over Time

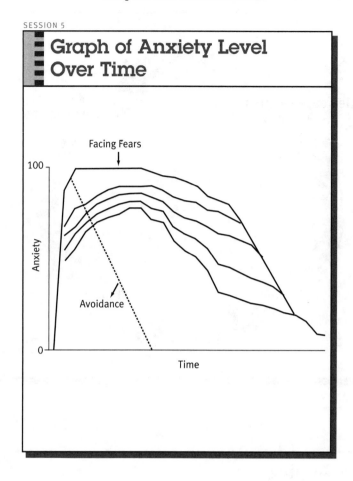

Frank's Fears
Realistic Versus Unrealistic ("False Alarm") Fears

Fears (circle the best response):

1. If I try out for the basketball team, then I might get cut.

   Realistic fear   Unrealistic fear

2. If I watch a scary movie, then the scary thoughts will never leave my head and bad things will happen.

   Realistic fear   Unrealistic fear

3. When I walk down the hall, kids may tease me.

   Realistic fear   Unrealistic fear

4. I'm struggling in math. If I don't study for the test, then I might fail.

   Realistic fear   Unrealistic fear

5. If I touch objects that other people touch, then I may get sick and die.

   Realistic fear   Unrealistic fear

6. If the news says there's a storm in the area, then there will be a tornado and something bad will happen.

   Realistic fear   Unrealistic fear

Frank's Realistic Fears

Realistic fears and interventions

1. If I try out for the basketball team, then I might get cut.
   Determine why Frank wants to join the basketball team. If it is for social reasons, determine whether basketball is the best social outlet or if there are other social activities Frank might be better suited to participate in. If it is for the sport, determine whether Frank's skills are best suited for basketball or another sport. Help coach Frank in that sport.

2. When I walk down the hall, kids may tease me.
   Alert teachers to teasing in the hallway and request that they increase their monitoring. Allow Frank to leave class 5 minutes early to transition before the halls become crowded. Teach Frank to ignore teasing.

3. I'm struggling in math. If I don't study for the test, then I might fail.
   Provide Frank with study guides and a math tutor. Provide accommodations (e.g., extra time, reduce number of problems).

Frank's Unrealistic Fears ("False Alarms")

Unrealistic fears and interventions

1. If I watch a scary movie, then the scary thoughts will never leave my head and bad things will happen.

2. If I touch objects that other people touch, then I may get sick and die.

3. If the news says there's a storm in the area, then there will be a tornado and something bad will happen.

Help Frank to identify the things that make him anxious. Teach Frank coping skills (i.e., tools to help him calm down). Gradually have Frank face his fears by progressing from his least feared situation to his most feared situation while coaching Frank to "use his tools." Reward courageous behavior. Remind Frank of the low probability that bad things will happen when he faces his fears. Over time, Frank will learn that he can handle the anxious feelings and that his anxiety goes down as he faces his fears.

My Child's Realistic and Unrealistic ("False Alarm") Fears

Realistic fears	Unrealistic fears
1.	1.
2.	2.
3.	3.
4.	4.
5.	5.

▐▐▐▐▐ Large Group

Activities

1. *Show and Tell:* Follow up here with anyone who has not yet participated in this activity.
2. *Deep breathing:* End the session with deep breathing. Each child can take a turn leading the group in this ritual.
3. *Closing/goodbye:* Give children prizes for sticker cards.

Assignments

1. Remind the group to schedule relaxation and other calming and/or relaxing activities throughout their week. Reward accordingly.
2. Finish the Active Minds and Helpful Thoughts series of worksheets.
3. Have parents talk with their spouses to update them on group progress.

END SESSION 5

Session Notes

_____

_____

_____

_____

_____

_____

_____

_____

_____

_____

_____

_____

_____

_____

_____

_____

More Mind–Body Connections

Introduction to Exposure

In Session 6, you will review some of the concepts introduced over the past sessions including "active minds," "helpful thoughts," and the use of deep breathing and other calming activities to decrease overall physiological arousal. Make sure to emphasize the connection between thoughts, feelings, and physical sensations. In this session, you will introduce the group to *graded exposure*—facing fears a little at a time. The parents and children will watch several videos over the next few sessions that illustrate children facing their fears. The group will continue to identify specific fears or situations for the children to face. Once the target situations or fears are identified, the children can begin to practice facing their fears both at home and in group.

SESSION STRUCTURE

- Large group, children and parents together
- Parent group and child group breakout sessions (occur simultaneously)
- Large group, parents and children together
- Parent–child pairs or trios
- Large group, children and parents together

SAMPLE SCHEDULE:
MORE MIND–BODY CONNECTIONS: INTRODUCTION TO EXPOSURE

- **Large Group** (15 minutes)
  - Snack
  - Discussion—review of schedule and/or updates and check-in with Show and Tell
  - Deep breathing

- **Child Group** (20–25 minutes)
  - Art activity
  - Active minds
  - Storytime

- **Parent Group** (20–25 minutes)

- **Large Group** (15 minutes)
  - Watch movie

- **Parent–Child Pairs or Trios** (25–30 minutes)
  - Learning to face fears
  - Facing my fear; picking a goal

- **Large Group** (5–10 minutes)
  - Prizes
  - Deep breathing

SOCIAL SKILLS

- Greeting others by name
- Sharing personal information in front of a group
- Increasing awareness about the connections among thoughts, physical feelings, emotions, and behavior
- Listening to others
- Asking questions and making comments during Show and Tell

Suggestions for Supporting Social Skills

- Encourage effort and any approximation toward participation, but do not force.
- Provide verbal and/or visual (use worksheets) prompts. (Parents and facilitators can provide these.)
- Model social skills.
- Use rewards for participation.

Large Group (Children and Parents Together)

Materials and/or Worksheets

- Snacks
- Written schedule
- Written list of rules, posted on the wall if necessary
- Pencils and/or markers

Goals

1. Children and parents will provide updates on calming activities and any completed Active Minds and Helpful Thoughts worksheets.
2. Children will continue to identify the connection between thoughts and feelings.

Activities

1. *Snack:* Provide a variety of drinks and snack foods for parents and children when they arrive for group.
2. *Discussion:* Get updates on relaxation: Were the children able to incorporate exercising, laughing, listening to music, and other relaxation and/or calming activities into their everyday life? Ask for a couple of positive examples. Also, ask if anyone experienced or identified any "false alarms" and, if so, how they handled them. If any of the children entered the "yellow" and/or "red" zones, ask how they were able to move from those zones to "green."
3. *Deep breathing:* Begin with deep breathing. Select one child to lead the group.

END—GROUP DIVIDES INTO PARENT GROUP AND CHILD GROUP

██████ Child Group

Materials and/or Worksheets

- This Is Me Relaxing… worksheet
- Active Minds and Helpful Thoughts worksheets
- Alarm Chain Reaction worksheets—optional
- Strategies for Calming Down and Facing Fears worksheet—optional
- Help Out Matthew worksheet
- What Can I Do to Help Myself? worksheet
- *More Parts* (Arnold, 2007)

Goals

1. Children will state the connection between thoughts and their bodies' physical reactions—thoughts can positively and/or negatively affect how they feel.
2. Children will show the group the Active Minds and Helpful Thoughts worksheets that they completed at home.
3. Children will draw a picture of themselves relaxing and/or engaging in a calming activity.

Activities

1. *Art activity:* Have children draw a picture of themselves relaxing and/or doing something calming. Use the This Is Me Relaxing… worksheet. This activity is included here to emphasize the importance of relaxing and/or calming activities.
2. *Active Minds and Helpful Thoughts revisited:* The children will share their completed Active Minds and Helpful Thoughts worksheets from home with the group. Encourage the children to state how they feel when their minds are "active" and how they feel when they are thinking "helpful thoughts." If the children do not have completed Active Minds and Helpful Thoughts worksheets, and if appropriate, you can complete a set of these worksheets together.
3. *Optional activity:* For children who understand the cognitive concepts conveyed in previous sessions, the series of Alarm Chain Reaction worksheets is highly recommended. The worksheets can be completed individually or together as a group. Now that the children have been introduced to the concept of *active minds* and the physical reactions of their bodies to anxiety, they can combine these concepts through this series of worksheets. If completed individually, remember to have share time.

   - On the first worksheet, Matthew (i.e., the boy who is afraid of snakes) experiences both increases in physical reactions to anxiety and many active thoughts. As the thoughts increase, so does Matthew's body's reaction to anxiety. The opposite also is true: As Matthew's body's reaction increases, so does his "active mind."
   - Next, the children will receive a My Alarm Chain Reaction worksheet to fill out regarding their own reactions to anxiety—both "active minds" and physical reactions. Use the attached list of suggestions, Alarm Chain Reaction! Strategies for Calming Down and Facing Fears, to help the children fill in the blanks. We have found that some children prefer general strategies that they can use across contexts (e.g., Telling themselves "I can handle this"), whereas other children do better with helpful thoughts that are as specific as possible (e.g., This is not a poisonous snake). Then the children will fill in the Help Out Matthew worksheet.
   - Finally, the children will fill out a What Can I Do to Help Myself? worksheet that shows them engaging in both relaxing and calming activities as well as thinking "helpful thoughts" as a way to reduce anxiety symptoms. Use the attached list of suggestions to fill in the worksheets.

4. *Storytime:* Read *More Parts* (Arnold, 2001) because of the connection between active minds and increased physical distress. Once again, pause at various points in the story to highlight "active minds" and "false alarms." If interested, some of the children may want to take turns reading the story.

END OF CHILD GROUP

On the next page, draw a picture of yourself relaxing.

What activity are you doing?

How does your body feel?

What are you thinking?

SESSION 6

This Is Me Relaxing . . .

I feel _____ I'm thinking_____

It's time to visit Matthew, the boy who is afraid of snakes, again. On the next page, you will see what happens to Matthew's body when he sees a snake at the zoo. His body alarm goes off, and his mind becomes active.

As Matthew begins to think more worried thoughts, his body alarm goes off even more!

After you read about Matthew, fill in your own **Alarm Chain Reaction** worksheet.

1. Pick a situation that makes you feel worried.

2. Write down how your body feels and what you think when you get worried.

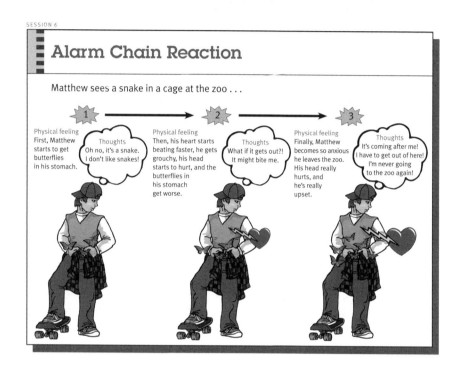

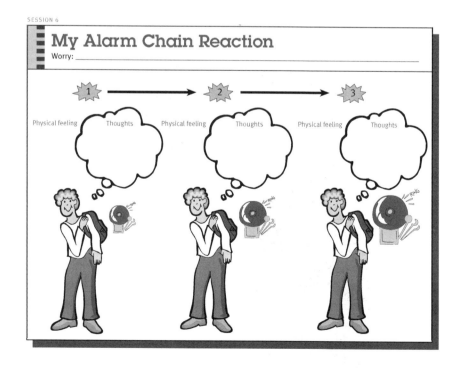

Help out Matthew

Write down what he could do to help his body's alarm chain reaction.
(Hint: Make sure to include calming activities and helpful thoughts.
You can use the **Strategies for Calming Down and Facing Fears** worksheet.)

1. _____

   _____

2. _____

   _____

3. _____

   _____

4. _____

   _____

5. _____

   _____

What Can I Do to Help Myself?

What could you do differently to help your body's alarm chain reaction?
(Hint: Make sure to include calming activities and helpful thoughts.
You can use the **Strategies for Calming Down and Facing Fears** worksheet.)

1. _____

_____

2. _____

_____

3. _____

_____

4. _____

_____

5. _____

_____

Strategies for Calming Down and Facing Fears

Suggestions for helpful thoughts:

- This is just a "false alarm."

- I can face my fear; nothing bad will happen.

- The worry feelings will go away.

- Fight back with facts.

- I can handle this.

- This is no big deal.

- Everyone makes mistakes.

- It's my worry bug; I can squash it!

Suggestions for calming activities:

- Take deep breaths.

- Go for a walk.

- Go outside.

- Ride my bike.

- Play with my pet.

- Read a book or magazine.

- Play video games.

- Watch television or a movie.

- Play with Lego set.

- Talk to someone.

- Play a game.

- Listen to music.

- Think about my favorite interest or activity.

Parent Group

Materials and/or Worksheets

- My Child's Realistic and Unrealistic ("False Alarm") Fears worksheet (from Session 5)
- Facing Fears through Exposure worksheet
- Alarm Chain Reaction worksheet (from Child Group)
- Steps to Success: Finding My Target Worksheet (blank and example)
- Steps to Success: Where Do We Begin? examples

Goals

1. Parents will identify a strategy for communicating information from the group to their spouses or partners.
2. Parents will encourage and reward their children for scheduling exercise, laughter, relaxation, and calming activities into their daily activities.

Activities

1. *Discussion:*

- Because we introduced many different concepts during the last session, we will need to review any questions covering the concepts of *adaptive protection, excessive protection,* and the *cycle of anxiety.*
- Next, review the My Child's Realistic and Unrealistic ("False Alarm") Fears worksheet with the parents and answer any questions they may have about differentiating between these concepts.
- Answer any questions the parents may have about helping their children schedule relaxing and/or calming activities as part of their daily routines.
- Highlight the connection between mind and body for both the parents and their children. Review the worksheets and/or activities from the children's group that emphasize this connection. Parents should be encouraged to work with their children to complete the Alarm Chain Reaction set of worksheets at home if their children do not complete them during group.
- Introduce the Facing Fears Through Exposure handout.
- Briefly review the Finding My Target worksheet and introduce the Steps to Success: Where Do We Begin? worksheets. These worksheets provide examples for how to get started facing fears. The Steps to Success: Where Do We Begin? sample worksheets offer a specific exposure hierarchy for several different fears. The introduction here will give parents a quick preview of what will be presented in the parent–child pairs or trios that follow. Encourage parents to refer back to these examples as they practice exposure with their children.
- *Note:* Emphasize the importance of remaining at any given exposure step until the child signals that he or she is ready to proceed to the next exposure step—it is very common to practice exposure steps over and over again to help children manage their anxiety at one step before moving on to the next.

END OF PARENT GROUP

Facing Fears Through Exposure

What is graded exposure? Graded exposure is the principle that gradual exposure to a feared situation or object will eventually reduce anxiety.

1. **Finding the target**

   • During the last session, you and your child used the stress-o-meter to select five fears and/or worries (or more) that interfere with your child's functioning at home or school or in the community (see examples) and listed them on the **Steps to Success: Finding My Target** worksheet. Looking at the fears and/or worries on that worksheet or on the **Fear Tracker** worksheet from the last session, ask your child which worry he or she would like to face first. Make sure the worry picked interferes with day-to-day functioning but that the anxiety is not so overwhelming to your child that he or she resists facing the fear. When completing the **Steps to Success: Finding My Target** worksheet, it is ok to have several fears listed at the same level (e.g., pretty big worry), rather than only listing one fear per level.

2. **Determining where to begin**

   • Using the **Steps to Success: Finding My Target** worksheet, take the target goal and create a series of steps that will lead to facing the fear. Write these steps from least anxiety producing (bottom of the ladder) to most anxiety producing (top of the ladder). It is sometimes helpful to identify the goal first and then, with your child, determine the small steps necessary to achieve the goal. All possible steps can be written separately on small cards and then put in order from easiest to hardest. This sequence can then be transferred to the **Steps to Success: Where Do We Begin?** worksheet.

   • Have your child select a reward that he or she will earn after facing his or her fear. You may provide mini rewards for each step of the ladder and a larger reward for completing all of the steps. Remember, you are rewarding effort in facing fears.

      • Help your child decide which strategies he or she will use as part of his or her plan. Write these down on the **Steps to Success: Where Do We Begin?** worksheet (see stress-o-meter). Examples include the following:

         • Handle your body's alarm reaction in an ongoing way (e.g., through exercise, deep breathing, and other calming activities).

(continued)

(continued)

Facing Fears
Through Exposure

- Think helpful thoughts (e.g., "Fight back with facts," "I can do this," "The worry will go away").

- Take advice from your friends (e.g., read a book, watch television, think of all the animals you can that begin with *b*, use a fidget toy).

3. Practicing at home

- Select the lowest step on the ladder; remind your child that anxiety goes away over time and that exposure and practice is a powerful tool.

- Continue practicing the first step until your child indicates that he or she is ready to move to the next step. This may take a number of practices until he or she feels ready. Reward your child's efforts and/or progress on this step, and then go to the next step up the ladder.

- Be empathic and convey confidence in your child's ability to face fears! Acknowledge to your child that you know that it may be hard to face his or her fears but you know he or she can do it and you will be there to help.

- Review the strategies your child will use in his or her overall plan to help handle the anxiety he or she feels when faced with specific situations or objects.

- Remind your child that anxiety goes up and down and it is his or her job to move from the red zone to the yellow zone and the yellow zone to the green zone on his or her stress-o-meter.

- Remember to praise your child, but also help your child praise him- or herself.

- You are ready to begin!

Steps to Success: Finding My Target

_____

Biggest worry

_____

Pretty big worry

_____

Medium worry

_____

Bit of a worry

_____

Not much of a worry

8

4

0

Steps to Success: Finding My Target

Home alone
Biggest worry

Ordering food in a restaurant
Pretty big worry

Making mistakes
Medium worry

Toilets flushing
Bit of a worry

Dogs
Not much of a worry

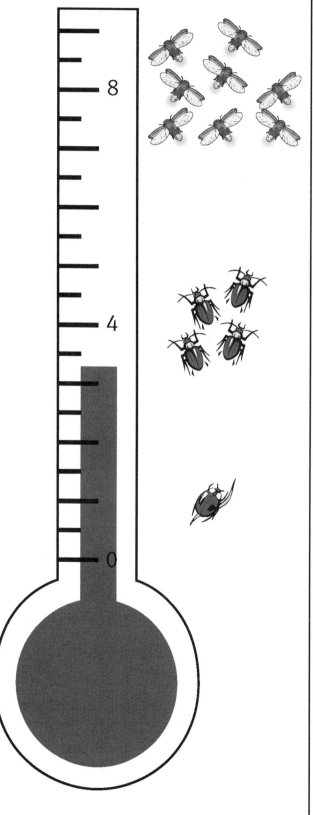

8

4

0

Steps to Success: Where Do We Begin?

What I'm working on (target goal): <u>Flushing toilet</u>

What I'm working for (bigger reward!): <u>Game boy game</u>

My reward for every exposure practice will be (small reward): <u>Piece of candy</u>

I will practice facing my fears (how often?): <u>Daily</u>

(Begin with Step 1 and move to Step 6)

6. <u>Go to a public bathroom and flush.</u>

5. <u>Stand by the toilet and flush.</u>

4. <u>Stand outside the stall while toilet flushes.</u>

3. <u>Stay in a public bathroom for 2 minutes.</u>

2. <u>Walk into a public bathroom for 1 minute.</u>

1. <u>Stand outside of a bathroom.</u>

Strategies for Success! What I can do to handle my worry and/or fear at home (e.g., deep breathing):

1. <u>Tell myself I can face this fear</u>

2. <u>Tell myself that my body is overreacting.</u>

3. <u>Breathe deeply.</u>

4. <u>Tell myself that toilets are loud but it does not mean anything bad will happen.</u>

YOU DID IT!

Steps to Success: Where Do We Begin?

What I'm working on (target goal): _Making mistakes_

What I'm working for (bigger reward!): _Bionicles_

My reward for every exposure practice will be (small reward): _Piece of candy_

I will practice facing my fears (how often?): _Daily_

(Begin with Step 1 and move to Step 6)

6. _Make one mistake on a spelling test._

5. _Make a mistake on math homework._

4. _Make a mistake writing the date on homework, do not erase, and turn in._

3. _Read a sentence out loud in small group and make a mistake with one of the words._

2. _Make a mistake while writing your name, erase only once, and then turn in the paper._

1. _Read a sentence out loud, and make a mistake reading one of the words in front of a parent._

Strategies for Success! What I can do to handle my worry and/or fear at home (e.g., deep breathing):

1. _Tell myself I can handle this._

2. _Tell myself that my body is having a "false alarm"!_

3. _Breathe deeply._

4. _Tell myself that everyone makes mistakes. It is no big deal!_

YOU DID IT!

Steps to Success: Where Do We Begin?

What I'm working on (target goal): <u>Ordering food in a restaurant</u>

What I'm working for (bigger reward!): <u>iTunes gift card</u>

My reward for every exposure practice will be (small reward): <u>A quarter</u>

I will practice facing my fears (how often?): <u>Daily</u>

(Begin with Step 1 and move to Step 6)

6. At a restaurant, order a Coke and all food items

5. At a restaurant, order a Coke and one other food item; have parents order additional foods.

4. At a sit-down restaurant, order a Coke, and say, "I'll have this," pointing to the menu.

3. At a sit-down restaurant, order a Coke, and have parents order any other food.

2. Order a Coke inside McDonald's.

1. Order a Coke at the McDonald's drive-through.

Strategies for Success! What I can do to handle my worry and/or fear at home (e.g., deep breathing):

1. Tell myself I can face this fear.

2. Tell myself I'm having a "false alarm" reaction.

3. Breathe deeply.

4. Tell myself I'm just ordering food; it's no big deal.

YOU DID IT!

Steps to Success: Where Do We Begin?

What I'm working on (target goal): <u>Being alone in the house</u>

What I'm working for (bigger reward!): <u>Movie night</u>

My reward for every exposure practice will be (small reward): <u>A quarter</u>

I will practice facing my fears (how often?): <u>Daily</u>

(Begin with Step 1 and move to Step 6)

6. <u>Stay in an upstairs room while Mom is in the basement for 5 minutes.</u>

5. <u>Stay in living room while Mom is up or down one level for 5 minutes.</u>

4. <u>Stay in living room while Mom is up or down one level for 3 minutes; call to her only one time.</u>

3. <u>Stand in the living room while Mom enters the adjoining Kitchen; Keep her in view.</u>

2. <u>Stand in the living room close to the doorway while Mom enters the adjoining Kitchen.</u>

1. <u>Walk with Mom from living room to Kitchen but don't stand next to her.</u>

Strategies for Success! What I can do to handle my worry and/or fear at home (e.g., deep breathing):

1. <u>Tell myself I can handle this.</u>

2. <u>Tell myself that my body is having a "false alarm"!</u>

3. <u>Breathe deeply.</u>

4. <u>Tell myself I can be away from Mom in the house—no problem!</u>

YOU DID IT!

▮▮▮▮▮ Large Group (Children and Parents Together)

Materials and/or Worksheets

- Instructional video: *Facing Your Fear: Dogs*

Goals

1. Children and parents will watch a video of a child facing his fear of dogs. The video emphasizes graded exposure and self-reward.

Activities

1. *Watch the video:* The group will watch a short video of a child facing his fear of dogs. A friend will coach the child to use CBT strategies while moving up the "steps to success" (stimulus hierarchy). Stop and start the video, asking the children to state the steps to facing fear. Write the following headings on poster board: 1) *Strategies to Help Worry and/or Anxiety* and 2) *Steps to Success* (to highlight graded exposure). Ask the children to identify each graded-exposure step and to identify the strategies that the coach in the video suggested to the boy who was facing his fear of dogs. Encourage the children to identify specific helpful thoughts as well as other strategies the boy used to help himself when facing fear (e.g., deep breathing). Write these down as you stop the video for each step. Following the video, the group will break into parent–child dyads and generate "steps to success" for two hypothetical situations.

> **Helpful Hint** Children often confuse "strategies" with the "steps to success." Remind them that *strategies* refer to tools or techniques for fighting or resisting their worries, such as deep breathing, helpful thoughts, or engaging in calming activities. *Steps to success* refer to specific exposure steps—facing fears a little at a time.

END—GROUP DIVIDES INTO PARENT–CHILD PAIRS OR TRIOS

▮▮▮▮▮ Parent–Child Pairs or Trios

Materials and/or Worksheets

- Fear Tracker worksheet (from last session)
- Facing Fear of Snakes at the Zoo worksheet
- Facing Fear of Talking in Class worksheet
- Steps to Success: Where Do We Begin? worksheet
- Pens, pencils, and/or markers
- Small index cards

Goals

1. Children/parents will complete Fear Trackers.
2. Children/parents will generate "steps to success" on several practice worksheets.
3. Children/parents will identify a goal and begin to write "steps to success" for the goals.
4. Children/parents will create a plan using tools to "fight" stress/upset/worry.
5. Children/parents will identify rewards for the children when they face fears.

Activities

1. *Fear Tracker:* Parents and children will quickly rate the child's fears on the Fear Tracker worksheet from last session.

2. *Introduction to exposure:* The children and their parents will complete two worksheets—Facing Fear of Snakes at the Zoo and Facing Fear of Talking in Class—that require them to generate steps to success for children facing their fears. It is important to differentiate between facing fears a little at a time (i.e., small, behaviorally defined steps that gradually increase exposure to the feared stimulus) and coping strategies or tools that the children may use to help them face fears (e.g., helpful thoughts, deep breathing). Have the children complete both worksheets if possible. If there is only time for one worksheet, however, have the children complete the Facing Fear of Snakes at the Zoo worksheet during group and finish up the Facing Fear of Talking in Class worksheet at home. Consider completing the first worksheet together as a group if the group works well together; otherwise, this activity can be completed in parent–child pairs.

3. *Getting started and putting it all together:* Use the worksheets Finding My Target (from last session) and Steps to Success: Where Do We Begin? The Steps to Success: Where Do We Begin? worksheet will include the child's goal, what he or she is working toward (reward), how often he or she will practice facing his or her fears, and what he or she can do to help with the worry and/or irritation (e.g., helpful thoughts, deep breathing, calming activities). The Steps to Success: Where Do We Begin? worksheet also includes space for the children to create steps to success, or a hierarchy for each individual worry, as well as a place for a sticker next to each step to indicate when a particular step has been mastered. Begin by identifying a clear goal. (The parent–child pairs may want to select worries and/or fears from the Fear Tracker in Session 5.) Then, using small index cards, ask the parents and children to create small behavioral steps that will help them achieve their goals (see examples). Rewards should be given for effort in facing fears. Make sure that the parent–child pairs write down how often they will practice facing their fears during the next week. Use the list of suggestions for helpful thoughts and calming strategies from the Alarm Chain Reaction activity referenced earlier in the session. For this session, you really just need to introduce these ideas to the group. They will complete their hierarchies during the next session so that by Session 8 they can begin facing fears in group.

Helpful Hint The children and their parents may disagree about where to begin. Children may select fears that their parents do not view as true fears. Similarly, parents may want to select fears that are highly problematic for their children and may underestimate the anxiety involved in facing that fear, making the children reluctant to tackle the fears that their parents have selected. It has been our experience that when we support the child's selection of a fear, at least initially, he or she is able to gain confidence in facing fears and can then work his or her way up toward facing more challenging fears. It may be difficult for several of the pairs or trios to complete this step during group. Try to identify at least an initial exposure step so that all group members can leave the group session with an identified goal and one step to practice at home. The parent–child pairs or trios can work on completing the remainder of the hierarchy on their own and/or bring back their work next session to go over with a facilitator.

Facing Fear of Snakes at the Zoo

Matthew wants to go on a field trip with his class to the zoo, but he is scared of snakes. Help him face his fear of snakes by creating **Steps to Success** and writing them on the lines below.

(Begin with Step 1 and move to Step 6)

6. _____

5. _____

4. _____

3. _____

2. _____

1. _____

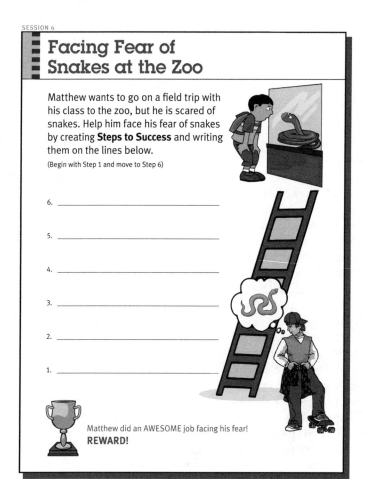

Matthew did an AWESOME job facing his fear!
REWARD!

Facing Fear of Talking in Class

Susie likes science but is afraid to talk in class. Help her face her fear of talking in class by creating **Steps to Success** and writing them on the lines below.

(Begin with Step 1 and move to Step 6)

6. _____

5. _____

4. _____

3. _____

2. _____

1. _____

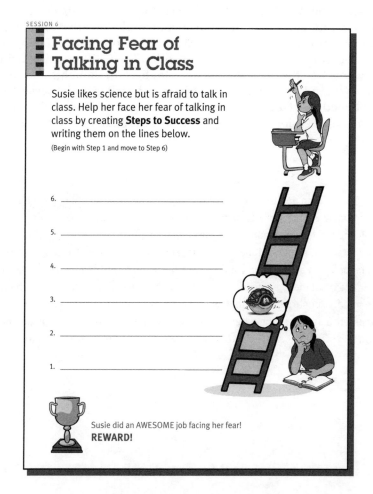

Susie did an AWESOME job facing her fear!
REWARD!

It may help to review your **Steps to Success: Finding My Target** and **Fear Tracker** worksheets to determine which fear to address first. Begin to write small steps that you can practice to help you face your fear and achieve your goal.

Next, talk with your mom or dad about what your reward will be when you reach the top of the ladder to success! What will you do to handle your worry when you are working on your goal and facing fears?

Steps to Success: Where Do We Begin?

What I'm working on (target goal): _____

What I'm working for (bigger reward!): _____

My reward for every exposure practice will be (small reward): _____

I will practice facing my fears (how often?): _____

(Begin with Step 1 and move to Step 6)

6. _____

5. _____

4. _____

3. _____

2. _____

1. _____

Strategies for Success! What I can do to handle my worry and/or fear at home (e.g., deep breathing):

1. _____

2. _____

3. _____

YOU DID IT!

4. _____

Assignments

1. Continue to brainstorm about the Steps to Success: Where Do We Begin? worksheet for one selected target, including strategies for implementation and handling worry and a reward system. Goal sheets will need to be completed by Session 8 when exposure begins during group.

2. If ready, practice exposure beginning with the first step indicated on the Steps to Success: Where Do We Begin? worksheet.

END—BACK TO LARGE GROUP FOR CLOSING

⫿⫿⫿⫿⫿ Large Group (Children and Parents Together)

Activity

1. *Closing/good-bye:* End with deep breathing and Show-and-Tell (if the children wish). Give children prizes for their sticker cards.

END SESSION 6

Session Notes

_____

_____

_____

_____

_____

_____

_____

_____

_____

_____

_____

_____

_____

_____

Introduction to Exposure

(Continued)

The purpose of Session 7 is to continue to introduce the group to graded exposure. The group will watch a second video today of a child facing his fears. The children and parents will complete the Steps to Success worksheet ladders, identifying specific fears or situations the children will face. Once these sheets are completed, the children can begin to practice handling their anxiety symptoms during group sessions as well as at home. The children will learn that they, too, will make *Facing Your Fears* videos. These segments will be filmed from Session 9 to Session 13.

SESSION STRUCTURE

- Large group, children and parents together
- Parent–child pairs or trios
- Parent group and child group breakout sessions (occur simultaneously)
- Large group, children and parents together

SAMPLE SCHEDULE: INTRODUCTION TO EXPOSURE (CONTINUED)

- **Large Group** (20–25 minutes)
  - Snack
  - Discussion—review of schedule and/or updates and check-in with Show and Tell
  - Deep breathing
  - Watch movie

- **Parent–Child Pairs or Trios** (20–25 minutes)
  - Fear Tracker
  - Practice facing fears

- **Child Group** (30 minutes)
  - How Did I Do?
  - Starting to make a movie

- **Parent Group** (30 minutes)

- **Large Group** (10 minutes)
  - Prizes and good-bye

SOCIAL SKILLS

- Greeting others by name
- Sharing personal information in front of a group
- Working cooperatively with others on a shared project (making *Facing Your Fears* videos)
- Complimenting each other on facing fears
- Listening to others
- Asking questions and making comments during Show and Tell

Suggestions for Supporting Social Skills

- Encourage effort and any approximation toward participation, but do not force.
- Provide verbal and/or visual (use worksheets) prompts. (Parents and facilitators may provide these.)
- Model social skills.
- Use rewards for participation.

▌▌▌▌▌ Large Group (Children and Parents Together)

Materials and/or Worksheets

- Snack
- Jar of special treats
- Written schedule
- Written list of rules, posted on the wall if necessary
- Pencils and/or markers
- Instructional video: *Facing Your Fears: Talking on the Phone*

Goals

1. Children and parents will provide updates on calming activities and any other homework assignments, including how they're doing with beginning to face fears.
2. Children and parents will watch a video of a child facing his fear of talking on the telephone, emphasizing graded exposure and self-reward.

Activities

1. *Snack:* Provide a variety of drinks and snack foods for parents and children when they arrive for group.
2. *Deep breathing:* Begin with deep breathing. Select one child to lead the group.
3. *Discussion:* This session will be the first real opportunity that children have to report on their experiences in facing fears. To add an extra incentive to engage in face-your-fears activities at home, children who report that they attempted to face their fears over the course of the week and/or engaged in relaxing and/or calming activities will be allowed to select a treat from the treat jar (very small pieces of candy and other treats).

   - Encourage the children and their parents to talk about their successes in incorporating calming and/or relaxing activities into daily routines.
   - Ask the parents and children about facing fears. Did they begin to practice their first steps? How did it go? If children do not respond, ask the parents what goals the children were able to accomplish over the course of the week.

4. *Watch the video:* The group will watch a short video of a child facing his fear of talking on the telephone. As with the dog phobia video, parents and children will generate the "steps to success" and "strategies to help worry and/or anxiety" that the child used in the video with help from his coach. Start and stop the video after every exposure step, discuss, and write responses down on large poster board. This is the second time that the children will be introduced to the concept of facing fears. After the video, before the group breaks into pairs, it is helpful to emphasize the importance of facing fears. You can engage the group in a short exercise by saying the following:

One of the best ways to face fears is to do the thing that you are afraid of. In this video, the boy was afraid of talking on the telephone, so he had to call people on the phone. So, if you are afraid of the dark you should _____ (wait for the children and/or parents to answer). If you are afraid of flying on an airplane, you should _____ . If you are afraid of heights, you should _____ . If you are afraid of talking to people you should _____ , and so forth.

END—GROUP DIVIDES INTO PARENT–CHILD PAIRS OR TRIOS

▄▄▄▄▄ Parent–Child Pairs or Trios

Materials and/or worksheets

- Steps to Success: Where Do We Begin? (from Session 6)
- Facing Fears Rating Sheet
- Pens, pencils, and/or markers
- Fear Tracker (from Session 5)
- Stress-o-meters
- Rewards for facing fears and/or participating in role plays

Goals

1. Parent–child pairs or trios will complete worksheets from last week, including Steps to Success.
2. Children will update fear ratings by using the Fear Tracker.
3. Parent–child pairs or trios will participate in role plays and/or real exposure of target goals.
4. Parent–child pairs or trios will reward each other for facing fears.

Activities

1. *Fear Tracker:* Parents and children will quickly complete the Fear Tracker.
2. *Putting it all together:* Parents and children will complete the worksheets Finding My Target (from last session) and Steps to Success: Where Do We Begin? The Steps to Success worksheet will include the child's goal, what he or she is working for (reward), graded exposure steps, how often he or she will practice facing her fears, and what he or she can do to help with the worry and/or irritation, including helpful thoughts and relaxation. This worksheet also includes space for the children to create a "steps to success" for each individual worry as well as to place a sticker next to each step to indicate when a particular step has been mastered. Rewards should be given for "facing fears," especially for the effort involved and

not necessarily for how successful the child has been. Make sure that the parent–child pairs or trios write down how often they will practice facing their fears during the next week.

3. *Practice role playing and/or in vivo exposure (if there is time):* Once the children and parents have selected goals for home and/or group and have generated exposure steps, the pairs or trios can enact a brief role play (see below), or if appropriate, they can face real fears via graded exposure in the clinic. Remind everyone that exposure is the most powerful tool. Anxiety goes away as time passes; therefore, exposure and practice staying in a fearful situation can be very powerful tools. We want to emphasize *facing your fears* as a critical tool. It is important to support parents as they coach their children to face fears. Each parent–child group can work with one facilitator, and the exposures can happen simultaneously if there are enough group facilitators. Alternatively, there is also value in two parent–child pairs or trios working together so that one child can practice his or her exposure in front of an "audience," thereby gaining the potential benefit of several different people praising his or her efforts. The outline for the role play might include the following:

- Identify the worry situation and several steps in facing fears. (This already should have been completed.)
- Identify one other person to share in role play.
- Identify two or more strategies for reducing anxiety.
- Identify who will play which part.
- Implement role play.
- It is important just prior to beginning the role play exposures or in vivo exposures that facilitators ask the children and parents where they are on their stress-o-meters. If the child rates him- or herself extremely high (i.e., in the "red" zone) on his or her stress-o-meter, then it would be important to determine whether the step is too difficult for the child; if so, it may be necessary to select an exposure step that is less difficult. Record each rating along with the specific fearful situation. Ask the child and/or parent for a rating postexposure to demonstrate that the anxiety decreases over time. Remember to reward the child's efforts and engagement in facing fears! The special jar of treats can be used here as well to reward in-session exposure practice. If real exposure is appropriate, several parent–child pairs can work together and coach each other to face fears.

Helpful Hint   It is extremely important that the Steps to Success: Where Do We Begin? worksheet is completed today. Some pairs or trios may finish this worksheet in enough time to practice an exposure in group. If so, one facilitator can help them get started. If not, the in-session exposure practice can begin next session. Some children may be reluctant to engage in the exposure practice. It is very important to include rewards as part of this practice. It is also very important to confirm that each child has a copy of the Steps to Success: Where Do We Begin? worksheet so that you can follow up on steps with parents in the upcoming week.

END—GO TO CHILD GROUP AND PARENT GROUP

Facing Fears Rating Sheet

Name: _____

Session: _____

Date: _____

Fear: _____

Step to complete today in facing fears: _____

_____

Reward for exposure practice: _____

	Child anxiety rating	Parent rates child anxiety
Before exposure		
During exposure		
Immediately after exposure		
5 minutes after exposure		

▐▐▐▐▐ Child Group

Materials and/or Worksheets

- Facing Fears: How Did I Do? worksheet
- Plan for My Movie worksheet
- Sample Script: Facing Your Fears
- Pens, pencils, and/or markers

Goals

1. The children will continue to learn the concepts of self-evaluation and self-reward.
2. The children will complete the *Facing Your Fears* script template for their own movies.

Activities

1. *Self-evaluation and self-reward:* Discuss the importance of self-evaluation and self-reward. It is especially important to emphasize rewarding *effort.* Say,

   After each of us faces a difficult situation, we need to look at how we handled facing our fears so we can learn from what went well and where we made mistakes.

   - Complete the Facing Fears: How Did I Do? worksheet for the child in the video we saw earlier. When did the child handle fear well, and when did he or she have difficulty? What could he or she do differently next time?

2. *Getting ready to make a movie:* The children will complete the Plan for My Movie! worksheet, which asks them to do the following: 1) identify a specific worry or fear, 2) identify "steps to success" or a stimulus hierarchy, 3) write a plan for reducing anxiety, 4) establish rewards for facing fears, 5) generate self-evaluation and self-reward comments, 6) determine what props they need, 7) decide on a setting, and 8) determine roles. Once this information has been completed, one of the facilitators will transfer the information to the *Facing Your Fears* script template and turn the contents into an episode of *Facing Your Fears.* Select one child who wishes to film his or her movie first. Make sure that his or her template is ready to go by the end of Session 8 so that a script can be written for Session 9. If appropriate, each child in the group will make his or her own *Facing Your Fear* videos. Filming for the videos will occur over the next 6 weeks. Explain that these videos are for them to keep after group is over to remind them of the strategies they used to face fears. Remember, a primary purpose of the video activity is to help the children internalize coping language and behavior via repetitive scripts and coping (rather than mastery) models for facing fears. A general script outline will be as follows:

   - Fearful child goes through the "steps to success" (stimulus hierarchy) while using coping statements and behaviors at the direction of a "coach" (can be either a friend or another actor).
   - The child is successful as he or she faces his or her fears and then rewards him- or herself with a desired prize when he or she has reached his or her goal.

   Each child will be responsible for one movie, including completing the template and identifying roles for everyone in the segment. Roles will include the following:

   - *Fear Facer:* Actor going through the "steps to success," facing his or her fears for the identified fearful situation
   - *Coach, helper bug, or friend:* Actor who supports and coaches the child through the "steps to success" hierarchy
   - *Narrator:* Actor who provides an introduction to the *Facing Your Fear* episode and explains throughout the segment how the child will conquer his or her fear

The children also may choose to identify "extras" for other parts during their segment, such as a parent, animal, peer, or teacher.

Helpful Hint   One script should be ready to begin filming in Session 9. However, all of the children can begin to write their templates and complete them over the next few sessions. If some children have difficulty generating ideas for the movie and/or if they are reluctant to share real fears, encourage them to write a video that they feel other children could benefit from watching. Remember to encourage the selection of fears that interfere with day-to-day functioning. Some children will be reluctant to act in the videos. Try to find a meaningful role for all of the group members, even if it is behind the camera (e.g., camera person, props). The scripts are intentionally repetitive to help the children generalize the key components in the intervention and to observe repeated positive coping.

END—BACK TO LARGE GROUP

Facing Fears: How Did I Do?

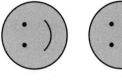
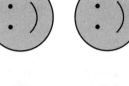

1. How well did I face my fears?

2. How well did I use my tools?

3. What will I do differently next time?

_____

_____

_____

Remember, look in your stress-o-meter to help you decide what to do next time!

Wow! Good job!

On the **Plan for My Movie** worksheet, you are going to choose your plot for your *own* movie!

Think about which of your worries you would like to target in your movie!

What will the steps to success be?
What will the plan be for calming down?
What will the reward be for facing your fear?

Where will your movie take place?
Who will the characters be?

Have fun planning your movie!

Plan for My Movie!

Specific worry or fear: _____

Steps to success
(facing fears a little at a time):

1. _____

2. _____

3. _____

4. _____

Strategies: (Hint: Make sure to
include calming activities and
helpful thoughts.)

_____

_____

_____

REWARDS! _____

_____

Self-praise:_____

_____

Props: _____

_____

_____

Setting: _____

_____

Roles:

1. Fear Facer: _____

2. Coach: _____

3. Narrator: _____

4. Other: _____

Sample Script:
Facing Your Fears:_____

Narrator: Greetings. In our *Facing Your Fears* segment today, we are going to help you conquer your fear of _____. We will introduce you to _____, who is afraid of _____. To help _____with his fear of _____, his friend _____ will coach him through the "steps to success." _____ will start with Step 1— _____ _____.

Child #1: Ok, I'm ready to face my fear of _____. I'll start by_____ _____.

Coach: Say, "I can do this—I want to beat this fear."

Child #1: I can do this. I want to beat this fear.

Coach: Where are you on your stress-o-meter?

Child #1: I'm starting to feel a little funny in my stomach; I think I'm at about a 6.

Coach: Try to get back down to a 4. Take a few deep breaths.

Child #1: (Takes a few breaths.)

Coach: Say, _____(provides suggestions for handling anxiety, such as helpful thoughts, and/or suggestions for calming/relaxing activities) _____ _____

Child #1: (Does suggestions) Now I think I am at about a 4.

Coach: Say, "I did it! Good for me, I finished the first step."

Child #1: I did it! Good for me, I finished the first step.

Narrator: (Child #1) _____'s next step is to _____ _____.

Child #1: I am ready to do the second step. I am ready to _____. I'm starting to feel a little worried.

Coach: Tell yourself, "Oh, it's just my worry bug again. I can fight this."

Child #1: Oh, it's just my worry bug again. I can fight this, but I feel like I am at a 7. Ahhh, I don't know what to do!

(continued)

(continued)

Sample Script:
Facing Your Fears:_____

Coach:	Take a few deep breaths.
Child #1:	(Pauses and takes three deep breaths.)
Coach:	You need to remember "helpful thoughts."
Child #1:	I am strong. _____ (Thinks helpful thoughts, such as "fight back with facts," or task-neutral thoughts). I know the worry feelings will go away. Hey, it's working. I feel better.
Narrator:	(Child #1) _____'s next step is to _____ _____.
Child #1:	I am ready to _____. This is the hardest part, and I'm having trouble doing this! I feel like yelling.
Coach:	Remember helpful thoughts. You can say, _____. Tell yourself the worry feelings will go away.
Child #1:	(Uses steps from plan.)
Child #1:	I did it! I am proud of myself for not freaking out. I think I am at a 3.
Narrator:	Now, (Child #1) _____'s final step is to _____.
Child #1:	Now it's time for my final step. I am going to face my fear of _____ and _____. Oh no, my worry is going up to an 8 this time.
Coach:	Say, "I can do this." You need to calm yourself down. Take three deep breaths.
Child #1:	I can do this. (Takes 3 deep breaths.) This will be over in a few minutes.
Child #1:	I did it. I faced my fear of _____ and my worry passed. I did a good job! I'm proud of myself. I think I'll reward myself with _____.
Coach:	Great job! (High five.)
Narrator:	Now, all of you have a plan for facing your fear of _____. I'll see you next time on another episode of *Facing Your Fears!*

‖‖‖‖‖ Parent Group

Materials and/or Worksheets

- None

Goals

1. Parents will review previously introduced concepts such as *steps to success* and *graded exposure.*
2. Parents will share successes as well as challenges in doing the graded exposures.
3. Parents will review guidelines for behaviors they can use when their children are engaged in graded-exposure tasks.

Activities

1. *Discussion:*

   - Review progress toward goals and answer any questions regarding the "steps to success," including exposure sessions, plans for reducing anxiety symptoms, use of reinforcement, and child self-evaluation and self-reward.
   - Create ongoing hierarchies and/or templates for hierarchies as each goal is attained. It may be best to list each child's name on a dry-erase board with his or her goal and the step on which he or she is currently working. Then brainstorm within a group context what next steps might be or what barriers might be preventing the child from moving on. It is important to be as specific as possible so that parents will walk away with a concrete plan. Make sure to keep notes on these steps or photocopy their hierarchy so that you can refer back to the exact steps the following week to track progress and/or struggles.
   - Use role playing with parents to demonstrate how they can work with their children. Review the following guidelines for parents to use when supporting their children:

     — Be empathic—state that you know how hard your child is working and that it is hard for him or her to face fears.
     — Ignore excessive anxiety symptoms.
     — Encourage and reinforce brave behavior.
     — Express confidence in your child's ability to handle fears.
     — Model courageous behaviors. Try to select situations that you have to handle but might feel a bit apprehensive in approaching. The situation can be real or an exaggerated situation for the child's benefit. In any case, it is important for you to make explicit the way you are coping so that your child understands that you also face fears.
     — Monitor your anxiety and/or any parenting style that might negatively affect your child.

   - Continue to help, support, and redefine the differences between realistic and/or unrealistic fears.
   - Review materials covered in the children's group, including the Facing Fears: How Did I Do? worksheet as well as the Plan for My Movie! worksheet.
   - Finally, it is important to talk briefly with the parents during the parent-only group about how they are sharing the information they are learning with their partners or other highly involved caregivers (e.g., grandparents). Are they noticing differences in how they respond to their children's worries compared with their spouse or partner? In other words, does one parent "push" while the other parent "nurtures"? It is important to acknowledge these roles with each other. This may be particularly important to discuss when separation anxiety disorder is present because parents may have very different ways of reacting to their child. Let them know other family members are invited to the final session—to view the videos the children made as well as for graduation.

Assignments

1. Parents and children will continue to work on facing fears; encourage practicing exposure every day.
2. Children will work on plans for their movies.

Helpful Hint You may want to address the tendency of some parents to either give in completely to their child's anxieties and fears or take the other extreme and become punitive (e.g., telling the child to "just knock it off"). Emphasize that it is very challenging to parent children with these concerns and that they need to remember the general guidelines as listed above.

END—BACK TO LARGE GROUP

‖‖‖ Large Group

Activity

1. *Closing/good-bye:* End with deep breathing. Give children prizes for their sticker cards.

END SESSION 7

Session Notes

_____

_____

_____

_____

_____

_____

_____

_____

_____

_____

_____

_____

Practicing Exposure and Making Movies

The purpose of Session 8 is for the parents and children to review the progress they have made thus far on selected target goals for home and to troubleshoot any difficulties. The families can discuss tools and/or strategies they have implemented for handling fears and/or worries that have worked particularly well as they have faced their fears. For Sessions 8–13, parents and children will begin each session with a brief exposure based on the goal that each child has identified. After the exposure has been completed, the children will complete their scripts and film their movies.

SESSION STRUCTURE

- Large group, children and parents together
- Parent–child pairs or trios
- Parent group and child group breakout sessions (occur simultaneously)
- Large group, children and parents together

SAMPLE SCHEDULE: PRACTICING EXPOSURE AND MAKING MOVIES

- **Large Group** (15 minutes)
  - Snack
  - Discussion—review of schedule and/or updates
  - Deep breathing

- **Parent–Child Pair or Trios** (25 minutes)
  - Fear Tracker
  - Practice facing fears

- **Child Group** (40 minutes)   ■ **Parent Group** (40 minutes)
  - Starting to make a movie

- **Large Group** (10 minutes)
  - Prizes and good-bye

SOCIAL SKILLS

- Greeting others by name
- Sharing personal information in front of a group

- Working cooperatively on a shared activity (filming *Facing Your Fears* videos)
- Complimenting and encouraging others for facing fears
- Listening to others
- Asking questions and making comments during Show and Tell

Suggestions for Supporting Social Skills

- Encourage effort and any approximation toward participation, but do not force.
- Provide verbal and/or visual (use worksheets) prompts. (These can be provided by parents and facilitators.)
- Model social skills.
- Use rewards for participation.

▌▌▌▌▌ Large Group (Children and Parents Together)

Materials and/or Worksheets

- Snack
- Jar of special treats
- Written schedule
- Written list of rules, posted on the wall if necessary
- Pencils and/or markers

Goals

1. Children and parents will provide brief updates on their "steps to success," making sure to include the tools that have been the most useful, such as the Active Minds and Helpful Thoughts worksheets, use of stress-o-meters, and relaxation.
2. Practice deep breathing in group. Try to have the children take turns leading each time.

Activities

1. *Snack:* Provide a variety of drinks and snack foods for parents and children when they arrive for group.
2. *Discussion:* As the children report on their progress, feel free to reward efforts at engaging in exposure practice and calming activities with a small treat from the special jar.

   - Obtain updates on steps to success, asking each child specifically if he or she had the chance to face his or her fear that week. Refer to your photocopied notes of their hierarchy. Once again, if children cannot respond or do not feel comfortable responding, ask their parents to help. In addition, ask about tools and strategies that have worked best for the children and calming and/or relaxing activities that they enjoy.
   - Ask the children and their parents to talk about facing fears, helping them distinguish between real fears and "false alarms."

3. *Deep breathing:* Select one child to lead the group.

END—GROUP DIVIDES INTO PARENT–CHILD PAIRS OR TRIOS

▮▮▮▮▮ Parent–Child Pairs or Trios

Materials and/or Worksheets

1. Completed goal sheets for each of the children
2. Facing Fear Rating Sheets (introduced in Session 7)
3. Facing Fears: How Did I Do? (introduced in Session 7)
4. Fear Tracker (from Session 5)
5. Stress-o-meters
6. Rewards for facing fears and/or participating in role plays

Goals

1. Parent–child pairs or trios will participate in role plays and/or real exposure to target goals.
2. Parent–child pairs or trios will reward each other for effort in facing fears.

Activities

1. *Fear Tracker:* Parents and children will quickly complete the Fear Tracker.
2. *Practice in vivo exposure:* At this point, the children and parents already have selected goals for home and/or group. The parent–child pairs or trios should begin to face real fears via graded exposure in the clinic. We believe that this is the heart of treatment and needs to be practiced live to ensure that parents are equipped with the skills they need to coach their children at home. If an in vivo exposure is not possible, role play the exposure. However, the use of role play should be considered the last resort. Remind everyone that exposure is the most powerful tool. Anxiety goes away as time passes; therefore, exposure and practice staying in a fearful situation can be very powerful tools. We want to emphasize *facing your fear* as a critical tool. Once the fears are identified, the children and their parents may enact a brief exposure task. It is important to support parents as they coach their children to face fears. The steps for the exposure should include the following:

   - Identify the worry situation and specific steps to face this fear. (This already should have been completed.)
   - Identify two or more strategies for reducing anxiety (plan to get green).
   - Identify coach (parent or therapist).
   - Identify reward for exposure practice.
   - Face your fear!

   Several parent–child pairs or trios can work together and coach each other to face fears or exposures can be done individually. Do not forget to take pre- and postexposure ratings for both parent and child using the stress-o-meter for each exposure. Also, make sure to include rewards for effort in facing fears and/or participating in role plays. Remember to complete the Facing Fears Rating Sheet for the activities and the Facing Fears: How Did I Do? worksheet.

END—GO TO PARENT GROUP AND CHILD GROUP

Facing Fears Rating Sheet

Name: _____

Session: _____

Date: _____

Fear: _____

Step to complete today in facing fears: _____

_____

Reward for exposure practice: _____

	Child anxiety rating	Parent rates child anxiety
Before exposure		
During exposure		
Immediately after exposure		
5 minutes after exposure		

Facing Fears: How Did I Do?

1. How well did I face my fears?

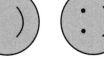

2. How well did I use my tools?

3. What will I do differently next time? _____

_____

_____

Remember, look in your stress-o-meter to help you decide what to do next time!

Wow! Good job!

135

▌▌▌▌▌ Child Group

Materials and/or Worksheets

- Completed *Facing Your Fears* script templates
- Props for filming
- Video camera and film
- Things to Think About While Filming Our Movies! worksheet

Goals

1. The children will finish their scripts.
2. The children will pull together props for one to two of the scripts.
3. The children will rehearse and film one movie.

Activities

1. *Script completion:* Continue to work on the templates during this time. One of the scripts will need to be ready for Session 9, so select the first script, assign roles, and gather and/or make all necessary props. Have the children review their Things to Think About While Filming Our Movies! worksheets as they are planning their movies.
2. *Unfinished business:* You need to determine what else should be completed for the next session. Whatever was not completed in group will need to be assigned; if necessary, templates can be returned via e-mail or fax midweek so that the facilitators can turn the template into an actual script.

Assignments

1. Finish templates for scripts, or e-mail them if necessary by midweek.
2. Collect and bring in props for the movies that will be filmed.

END—BACK TO LARGE GROUP

Things to Think About While Filming Our Movies!

Goals

How are you doing on your *goals* at home?
Keep at it! You're doing great!

Relax and have fun

Are you planning fun activities and time to relax? Try to plan some fun things to do during the week and calming or relaxing activities.

Are you ready to *film* your movie?
Do you need props? What else do you need?

Filming

Have fun with your movies, and good luck with your goals at home!

‖‖‖ Parent Group

Materials and/or Worksheets

- None

Goals

1. Increase the parent's ability to identify appropriate target behaviors for intervention.
2. Review the components of the intervention program, such as identifying target behaviors, differentiating between realistic and unrealistic fears, creating "steps to success," learning about graded exposure and rewards, using self-evaluation and self-reward, and coaching children through exposure sessions.
3. Identify ways that parents will be communicating with spouses and/or caregivers.
4. Address relapse prevention.

Activities

1. *Discussion:*

   - Review each child's progress toward at-home goals, including frequency of exposure and/or practice sessions and corresponding plans for reducing anxiety symptoms.
   - Revise the exposure hierarchy and brainstorm new hierarchies as needed. As described previously, it is helpful to brainstorm the next steps for hierarchies on a whiteboard, then write down and photocopy the steps to make sure each family knows the next steps for their child. Emphasize the importance of *daily* exposure practice.
   - As new hierarchies are created, you may need to teach complementary social skills that may be essential in achieving target goals. For example, some fears may be primarily social, such as talking to unfamiliar peers. If this is the case, in addition to a hierarchy, it also is important to directly teach the child the skills that are necessary when approaching a peer.
   - Troubleshoot common problems.
   - Highlight moments throughout the week that have gone well. Have families share their successes.
   - Address communication between the parent attending the group and his or her spouse and/or other caregivers.
   - Prevent relapse. Begin to discuss families' worries once group ends; emphasize the importance of practicing the core elements of *Facing Your Fears*—"false alarms," relaxation and/or calming activities, active minds and helpful thoughts, and facing fears a little at a time—to handle future symptoms. Remind families how to identify new target behaviors and face new fears. Tell them that there will be a booster session approximately 4–6 weeks after the final session. Continue to address these issues throughout the remainder of the sessions.

Assignments

1. Parents and children will continue to work on in-home goal.
2. Parents and children will continue to build calming and/or relaxation activities into their everyday routines.

Helpful Hint It is essential that the parents understand the importance of exposure practice and hierarchies and can support their children as they practice exposure on a daily basis. It is also important to talk to families about the slow or even limited progress if exposure is not included as part of the intervention. At the beginning of each group session, care and attention is given to each child's successes and efforts at facing fears; when the children discuss their exposure practice, facilitators may praise and applaud all positive progress.

END—BACK TO LARGE GROUP

▸▸▸▸▸ Large Group (Children and Parents Together)

Activity

1. *Closing/good-bye:* End with deep breathing and prizes.

END SESSION 8

Session Notes

_____

_____

_____

_____

_____

_____

_____

_____

_____

_____

_____

_____

_____

_____

_____

Facing Fears and Making Movies

The purpose of Sessions 9–13 is to practice facing fears via role-play and/or exposure activities in the clinic. Filming will continue.

SESSION STRUCTURE

- Large group, children and parents together
- Parent–child pairs or trios
- Parent group and child group (occur simultaneously)
- Large group, children and parents together

SAMPLE SCHEDULE: FACING FEARS AND MAKING MOVIES

- **Large Group** (15 minutes)
  - Snack
  - Discussion—review of schedule and/or updates
  - Deep breathing

- **Parent–Child Pairs or Trios** (20–25 minutes)
  - Fear Tracker
  - Practice facing fears

- **Child Group** (40–45 minutes)   ■ **Parent Group** (40–45 minutes)
  - Starting to make a movie

- **Large Group** (10 minutes)
  - Prizes and good-bye

SOCIAL SKILLS

- Greeting others by name
- Sharing personal information in front of a group
- Working cooperatively on a shared activity (making videos)
- Complimenting and encouraging others for facing fears
- Listening to others
- Asking questions and making comments during Show and Tell

Suggestions for Supporting Social Skills

- Encourage effort and any approximation toward participation, but do not force.
- Provide verbal and/or visual (use worksheets) prompts. (These can be provided by parents and facilitators.)
- Model social skills.
- Use rewards for participation.

▋▋▋▋ Large Group (Children and Parents Together)

Materials and/or Worksheets

- Snack
- Jar of special treats
- Written schedule
- Written list of rules, posted on the wall if necessary
- Pencils and/or markers

Goals

1. Children and parents will provide brief updates on homework, assignments, and their plan for the day.
2. Practice deep breathing in group. Try to have the children take turns leading each time.

Activities

1. *Snack:* Provide a variety of drinks and snacks for the parents and children when they arrive for group.
2. *Discussion:* Obtain updates on how goals are going, including homework assignments (this also can be discussed in the parent group). Reward efforts to face fears with a treat from the special jar. Go over the schedule for today—the children will continue filming today.

END—GO TO PARENT–CHILD PAIRS OR TRIOS

▋▋▋▋ Parent–Child Pairs or Trios

Materials and/or Worksheets

- Completed goal sheets for each of the children
- Fear Tracker (from Session 5)
- Facing Fears: How Did I Do? (introduced in Session 7)
- Facing Fears Rating Sheets (introduced in Session 7)
- Stress-o-meters
- Rewards for facing fears and/or participating in role plays

Goals

1. Parent–child pairs or trios will participate in role plays and/or real exposure of target goals.
2. Parent–child pairs or trios will reward each other for effort in facing fears.

Activities

1. *Fear Tracker:* Parents and children will quickly complete the Fear Tracker.
2. *Practice in vivo exposure:* The parent–child pairs or trios should face real fears via graded exposure in the clinic. Do not forget to support parents as they coach their children to face fears. As the families understand these concepts, they can coach each other. As before, if a live exposure cannot occur for whatever reason, you can role-play the exposure instead. The steps for the exposure should include the following:

   • Identify the worry situation and specific steps to face this fear. (This already should have been completed.)
   • Identify two or more strategies for reducing anxiety (plan to get green).
   • Identify coach (parent or therapist).
   • Identify reward for exposure practice.
   • Face your fear!

Several parent–child pairs or trios can work together and coach each other to face fears. Remember to do pre- and postexposure ratings for both the parent and child and to include rewards for facing fears and/or participating in role plays. Remember to complete the Facing Fear Rating Sheet worksheet and the Facing Fears: How Did I Do? worksheet for the activities.

END—GO TO CHILD GROUP AND PARENT GROUP

Facing Fears Rating Sheet

Name: _____

Session: _____

Date: _____

Fear: _____

Step to complete today in facing fears: _____

_____

Reward for exposure practice: _____

	Child anxiety rating	Parent rates child anxiety
Before exposure		
During exposure		
Immediately after exposure		
5 minutes after exposure		

Facing Fears: How Did I Do?

1. How well did I face my fears?

2. How well did I use my tools?

3. What will I do differently next time? _____

_____

_____

_____

Remember, look in your stress-o-meter to help you decide what to do next time!

Wow! Good job!

▐▐▐▐▐▐ Child Group

Materials and/or Worksheets

- Completed templates for scripts
- Props for filming
- Video camera and film

Goals

1. The children will pull together props for one to two of the movies.
2. The children will rehearse and film one movie.

Activities

1. *Rehearsal and filming:* Begin to film one movie today.
2. *Unfinished business:* You need to determine what else needs to be completed for the next session. Whatever was not completed in group will need to be assigned; if necessary, templates can be returned via e-mail or fax midweek so that the facilitators can turn the template into an actual script.

Assignments

1. Collect and bring in props for the additional scripts that have not yet been filmed.

Helpful Hint This may be a very fun but challenging activity. The children are alternately quite excited and anxious when filming, typically. It may be helpful to practice one scene, then film one scene. Have the children read their scripts. Remember that you will have more sessions to complete filming.

END—BACK TO LARGE GROUP

┃┃┃┃┃ Parent Group

Materials and/or Worksheets

- None

Goals

1. Increase the parent's ability to identify appropriate target behaviors for intervention.
2. Review the components of the intervention program, such as identifying target behaviors, differentiating between realistic and unrealistic fears, creating steps to success, learning about graded exposure plus rewards, using self-evaluation and self-reward, and coaching children through exposure sessions.

Activities

1. *Discussion:*

   - Review each child's progress toward at-home goals, including frequency of exposure and/ or practice sessions and corresponding plans for reducing anxiety symptoms.
   - Revise the exposure hierarchy and brainstorm new hierarchies as needed.
   - Troubleshoot common problems.
   - Highlight moments throughout the week that have gone well. Have families share their successes.
   - In Session 13, remind parents that there is only one group meeting remaining. Spouses and/ or siblings are invited to attend the final session, if appropriate, to share in the children's successes and to better understand the exposure steps so that all family members can continue to support the child in facing fears. It may be stressful to have an exceptionally large group of participants for this final session, so it will be important to prepare the children and have them identify strategies that will help them stay calm.
   - Ask parents if they would like to bring one treat to share with the group for the final session.
   - Prevent relapse. Continue to discuss families' worries once group ends. Emphasize the importance of practicing the core elements of *Facing Your Fears*—"false alarms," relaxation and/or calming activities, active minds and helpful thoughts, and facing fears a little at a time—to handle future symptoms. Remind children how to identify new target behaviors and face new fears. Ask about scheduling a booster session. Continue to address these issues throughout the remainder of the sessions.

Assignments

1. Parents and children will continue to work on in-home goals.
2. Parents and children will continue to build calming/relaxation activities into everyday routines.
3. Parents will continue to model courageous behaviors.

END—BACK TO LARGE GROUP

⚎ Large Group (Children and Parents Together)

Activity

1. *Closing/good-bye:* End with deep breathing, positive mantras, and prizes.

END SESSIONS 9–13

Session Notes

_____

_____

_____

_____

_____

_____

_____

_____

_____

_____

_____

_____

_____

_____

_____

Graduation

The purpose of the final session is to review lessons learned, show the movies that the children filmed, complete any final assessments, and talk about relapse prevention.

SESSION STRUCTURE

- Large group, children and parents together
- Parent group and child group breakout sessions (occur simultaneously)
- Large group, children and parents together

SAMPLE SCHEDULE: GRADUATION

- ■ **Large Group** (20–25 minutes)
  - Snack
  - Introductions
  - Discussion of schedule and updates
  - Fear Tracker worksheet
  - Picture taking
  - Deep breathing

- ■ **Child Group** (25 minutes)   ■ **Parent Group** (25 minutes)
  - Storytime
  - Time spent worrying now
  - Favorite tools

- ■ **Large Group** (35–40 minutes)
  - Watching movies
  - Lessons learned
  - Graduation and awards
  - Prizes and good-bye

SOCIAL SKILLS

- Greeting others by name
- Sharing personal information in front of a group

- Watching themselves on videos in front of an audience
- Complimenting others for facing fears
- Listening to others
- Asking questions and making comments during Show and Tell

Suggestions for Supporting Social Skills

- Encourage effort and any approximation toward participation, but do not force.
- Provide verbal and/or visual (use worksheets) prompts. (These can be provided by parents and facilitators.)
- Model social skills.
- Use rewards for participation.

Large Group (Children and Parents Together)

Materials and/or Worksheets

- Fear Tracker worksheet (from previous sessions)
- Jar of special treats

Goals

1. Review today's plan.
2. Introduce other family members.
3. Take a group photo of the children.

Activities

1. *Snack:* Families will have brought snack foods, so begin the group with snack time.
2. *Introductions:* Because guests will be attending the group today, have everyone go around the room and introduce themselves.
3. *Updates on progress:* Children and their parents may want to share continued successes. Reward with treats when appropriate.
4. *Review the schedule:* Because it is the last session and guests will be attending the group, the children may be distracted; direct them to the day's schedule.
5. *Fear Tracker worksheet:* Ask parents and children to quickly rate their fears.
6. *Picture taking:* Take a few group photos. If the children brought cameras, they can take pictures as well.
7. *Deep breathing:* End the large group with deep breathing, and then have the children and parents break into their respective groups.

END—GO TO PARENT GROUP AND CHILD GROUP

Parent Group

Materials and/or Worksheets

- None

Goals

1. Parents will ask any final questions.

Activities

1. *Discussion:* Answer any final questions, and discuss how the parents might keep in touch with each other informally.
2. *Relapse prevention:* Facilitators and parents will continue to review core concepts and troubleshoot future difficulties.
3. *Schedule the booster session* (4–6 weeks after the final session).

END—BACK TO LARGE GROUP

Child Group

Materials and/or Worksheets

*   *Parts* (Arnold, 1997) or *More Parts* (Arnold, 2001)
*   How Much Time Do You Spend Worrying Now? worksheet
*   My Favorite Tools worksheet

Goals

1. Children will read a favorite book and discuss the connection between thoughts, feelings, and behavior.
2. Children will report how much time they spend worrying now.

Activities

1. *Storytime:* Read either the book *Parts* (Arnold, 1997) or *More Parts* (Arnold, 2001) if the children indicated that they enjoyed this series. Emphasize the connection between thoughts and "false alarm" reactions. Active minds can make "false alarm" reactions worse, and helpful thoughts can make "false alarm" reactions better.
2. *Time spent worrying:* The children also need to complete the worksheet that they originally completed at the beginning of group—How Much Time Do You Spend Worrying Now? Discuss with the children how much time they spend worrying now compared with the time spent worrying when the group first started.
3. *My favorite tools:* Discuss as a group all of the tools and strategies for handling worry, and have the children select their favorites—what they think they'll use the most when facing fears. Have the children use the My Favorite Tools worksheet to document the tools they find most useful.
4. *Follow-up and relapse prevention:* The children will talk with each other about how they will stay in touch, predict future difficulties, and remind the group of core concepts.

END—BACK TO LARGE GROUP

How Much Time Do You Spend Worrying Now?

Write down your worries here!

Fun time

Worry time

Time I spend worrying

Me

A little

Some

A lot!

In group, you learned a lot of different strategies for facing fears or worry. Some of these strategies may work better than others. On the next page, write down your favorite tools for facing fears and handling worry.

My Favorite Tools

Calming and/or relaxing activities

_____

_____

_____

_____

Helpful thoughts

_____

_____

_____

_____

I faced fears by . . .

_____

_____

_____

_____

_____

‖‖‖‖‖ Large Group

Materials and/or Worksheets

- Lessons I Learned in Group worksheet
- Movies (Facing Your Fears)
- Graduation certificates
- Acting awards

Goals

1. Children and parents will review the Lessons I Learned in Group worksheet during group.
2. The families will watch the movies.
3. The children will participate in the graduation ceremony and receive awards.

Activities

1. *Movies:* Watch the Facing Your Fears movies as a group and provide copies of the movies on DVD to everyone.
2. *Lessons learned:* Review the Lessons I Learned in Group worksheet. Children and parents can take turns reading sentences out loud. The Lessons I Learned in Group worksheet in the manual should be used only as a template. It is important to individualize the worksheet for the particular group to include each child's favorite interests and individual successes.
3. *Graduation and awards:* Present the children with graduation certificates as well as awards for acting roles (e.g., best narrator, best worrier, best coach).
4. Final good-bye.

END SESSION 14—AND GROUP

Session Notes

_____

_____

_____

_____

_____

_____

_____

_____

Lessons I Learned in Group

- We all use different words for worry—*scared, anxious, nervous,* and *freaked out* are some of them.

- When we worry too much, it can make it hard for us to have fun, do well in school, or get along with our family or friends.

- Different things make each of us worry or feel anxious. It may be a fear of the dark, of going outside, of staying home alone, or of talking to people.

- We can show worry or anxiety in lots of different ways, such as getting really quiet, leaving the room, crying, getting silly, or even having our bodies shake.

- Sometimes our worry is a "false alarm"—our bodies may feel upset, then our minds get really active and we start thinking all sorts of thoughts that make us worry more.

- It helps to know the kinds of situations that make us worry so we can get ready to fight it!

(continued)

(continued)

Lessons I Learned in Group

- We can do *lots* of things to get rid of worry. We can do relaxing and calming things like taking deep breaths, telling a joke, or going for a walk. We also can remember that helpful thoughts can make our bodies calm down. We can fight back with facts or tell ourselves that the worry feelings will go away. We can watch our favorite television shows, play video games, listen to music, ride bikes, read a book, or talk on the phone while we wait for our worry to go away.

- We are all very strong and tough. We can beat worry!

- Most important, we learned that the best way to get rid of worry is to face fears!

Favorite things I'll remember about my friends:

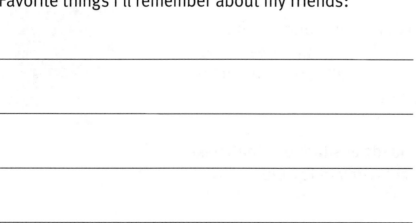

_____

_____

_____

_____

We learned a whole lot of different things in group!

Booster Session

The purpose of the booster session is to get reacquainted briefly with the group members, talk about what they have been doing to face their fears over the past several months, and obtain examples of any successes they may have had in facing their fears. We will review basic concepts from the group and help the parents and children apply these concepts to any current anxiety-provoking situations. Another primary purpose of the booster is to encourage and remind parents and children to use strategies they have learned in group (e.g., helpful thoughts, calming activities) to face new fears.

SESSION STRUCTURE

- Large group, children and parents together
- Parent–child pairs
- Parent group and child group breakout sessions (occur simultaneously)
- Return to large group for closing

SAMPLE SCHEDULE: BOOSTER SESSION

- ■ **Large Group** (20–25 minutes)
  - Snack
  - Discussion—catching up
  - Deep breathing

- ■ **Parent–Child Pairs or Trios** (20–25 minutes)
  - Current worries
  - Fear Tracker worksheet
  - Identify new goals
  - Favorite tools
  - Share time

- ■ **Parent Group** (30–35 minutes)

- ■ **Child Group** (30–35 minutes)
  - Movie
  - Problem-solving fears

- ■ **Large Group** (10 minutes)
  - Prizes and good-bye

SOCIAL SKILLS

- Greeting others by name
- Sharing personal information in front of a group

- Complimenting others on progress in facing fears
- Listening to others
- Asking questions and making comments during Show and Tell

Suggestions for Supporting Social Skills

- Encourage effort and any approximation toward participation, but do not force.
- Provide verbal and/or visual (use worksheets) prompts. (These can be provided by parents and facilitators.)
- Model social skills.
- Use rewards for participation.

▮▮▮▮▮ Large Group (Children and Parents Together)

Materials and/or Worksheets

- Snacks
- Jar of special treats
- Written schedule
- Written list of rules, posted on the wall if necessary

Goals

1. Children and their parents will talk about recent fun activities in which they have participated.
2. Children and their parents will provide several examples of how they have faced their fears.

Helpful Hint   This may be the first contact that the children have had with each other in quite a while, so they may need a little time to warm up and get used to being with each other again. Be prepared for silly, agitated, and/or withdrawn behaviors.

Activities

1. *Snacks:* Provide a variety of drinks and snack foods for parents and children when they arrive for group.
2. *Discussion:* Use the special jar of treats to reward facing fears and engaging in relaxing and/or calming activities.

   - Deep breathing: Begin with deep breathing. One child may want to lead the group. Emphasize belly breathing.
   - Catching up: Group members will take turns talking about what they have been doing over the past several weeks and/or months since the last group meeting. They can emphasize fun and/or interesting activities.
   - Facing fears updates: The facilitators will encourage each parent–child pair or trio to quickly generate two examples of how the children have faced fears in recent weeks and/or months and what strategies they used to help them. Ask the groups to provide examples that fall into one of four main categories (these should be written on the board)—recognizing "false alarms," helpful thoughts, calming and/or relaxing activities, and facing fear a little at a

time. When the pairs or trios are ready to share with the group, the facilitators can write these examples on the poster board so everyone can see each other's successes.

END — GROUP DIVIDES INTO PARENT–CHILD PAIRS OR TRIOS

Parent–Child Pairs or Trios

Materials and/or Worksheets

- My Checklist of Fears, Worries, and Irritations worksheet
- Steps to Success: Finding My Target worksheet
- Fear Tracker worksheet (from Session 5)
- My Favorite Tools worksheet
- Pens, pencils, and/or markers
- Fresh sticker cards and stickers

Goals

1. Children and parents will identify the situations or things that are currently problematic and put them in order according to the level of the severity of the symptoms.
2. Children, with help from their parents, will identify their favorite tools for handling worry and/or anxiety.

Activities

1. *Current worries:* To get a sense of the current worries, parents and children will first complete the My Checklist of Fears, Worries, and Irritations worksheet. It would be most helpful for the pairs or trios also to include an anxiety rating (on a scale of *1–8*) to measure level of anxiety for the situations selected.
2. *Fear Tracker worksheet:* Parents and children can review their Fear Tracker worksheets and complete as appropriate.
3. *Finding a new target:* At this point, the facilitators do not know the extent to which the children will identify any problematic behaviors. Should they identify some anxiety symptoms, ask the pairs or trios to transfer the worries to a Finding My Target worksheet so that they can continue to address symptoms at home after the booster session.
4. *Identifying effective tools:* Children and their parents will next list the kinds of activities, tools, and strategies that they have implemented since group that they have found to be the most helpful. They will complete the My Favorite Tools worksheet as a way to summarize these strategies. Help the group generate tools for the following categories: calming and/or relaxing activities, helpful thoughts, and facing fears a little at a time (children may explain how they gradually approached a fearful situation). Encourage the children to write down times when they have recognized "false alarms."
5. *Share time:* When the parent–child pairs or trios have completed the forms, encourage each pair to share their worksheets with another pair or trio. (If appropriate, share time can occur in the large group instead.)

Helpful Hint   The children may be very excited to see each other again and may have some difficulty in engaging in these activities. Keep in mind that these activities are intended as *suggestions* for structure. Flexibility is the key for this session.

END — GROUP DIVIDES INTO PARENT GROUP AND CHILD GROUP

My Checklist of Fears, Worries, and Irritations

I'm afraid of, worried about, or irritated about . . .

	No	Sometimes	A lot	Stress-o-meter rating (1–8)
Being late				
Being home alone				
Making mistakes				
The dark				
Letting go of past events				
Dogs and/or cats				
Storms and/or tornados				
Bugs, spiders, and/or bees				
Getting a disease				
Being teased				
Germs				
Trying new foods				
Being away from family				
Using public bathrooms				
Talking to new people				
Talking in school				
Getting to sleep				
Scary movies				
Changes				
Asking for help				
Parents going out				
Getting lost				
Dying				
Starting homework				
World events				
Going to someone's house				
Loud noises				
Heights				
Starting a conversation				
Being in a room by myself				
Performing in front of others				
Other:				

You have worked hard to face your fears, but you may still have worries that get in your way of having fun or getting things done. Review the list on the next page and answer the following questions:

Which of these items do you worry about sometimes?
Which do you worry about a lot?
Which items do you never worry about?

After you read the list, decide with your mom or dad which kinds of things you continue to worry about. Transfer them to the **Steps to Success: Finding My Target worksheet**. If you do not have any big worries now, then you can leave this worksheet blank.

Steps to Success: Finding My Target

Biggest worry

Pretty big worry

Medium worry

Bit of a worry

Not much of a worry

In group, you learned a lot of different strategies for facing fears or worry. Some of these strategies may work better than others. On the next page, write down your favorite tools for facing fears and handling worry.

My Favorite Tools

Calming and/or relaxing activities

_____

_____

_____

_____

Helpful thoughts

_____

_____

_____

_____

I faced fears by . . .

_____

_____

_____

_____

╻╻╻╻╻╻ Parent Group

Materials and/or Worksheets

- None

Goals

1. Parents will provide information on the progress made over recent weeks and/or months.
2. Parents will identify any current areas of concern.
3. Parents will review the steps involved in the intervention program for anxiety symptoms as well as identify their role in the treatment process.
4. Parents will work together and generate solutions for one to two problems.

Activities

1. *Discussion:*

   - Obtain updates from the parents with regard to progress as well as continued concerns.
   - Identify a few concerns and troubleshoot as examples for the group because there probably will not be enough time to problem-solve for each family. If there are multiple concerns, consider dividing the parents into groups, working on several problems at one time, and then sharing the results with the larger group. The facilitators will likely need to help families distinguish between realistic and unrealistic fears and remind parents how to create hierarchies.

> **Helpful Hint**   The purpose of the booster is to remind parents that for dealing with true anxiety symptoms, the basic approach is essentially the same framework that they were originally introduced to at the beginning of the group. When problem-solving as a group, try to select one or two concerns that may be universal for all group members to use as examples. If there are no major concerns in handling anxiety symptoms, open the discussion up to talking about other concerns the group may have (e.g., school-related issues).

END—BACK TO LARGE GROUP

╻╻╻╻╻╻ Child Group

Materials and/or Worksheets

- Videorecorded episode of *Facing Your Fears: Getting Stuck in a Store that Is Closing*
- Poster paper, pens, markers
- Large drawings of "stressed" boy and "calm" boy (see Stressed to Calm worksheet)
- Common anxiety-provoking situations written on slips of paper
- Deck of cards with suggestions for helpful thoughts, calming and/or relaxing activities, and graded exposure

Goals

1. Children will review an episode of *Facing Your Fears* and complete the following:
    - Write down the "steps to success."
    - Write down the strategies that the child used in the video (e.g., helpful thoughts, calming and/or relaxing activities).
    - Write down what the coach said to the child.
    - Write down how the child rewarded himself.

Activities

1. *Video activity:* The group will watch a videorecording of a child facing his fear of stores closing. As in previous videos, a friend will coach the child to use strategies while moving up the "steps to success" (stimulus hierarchy). Stop and start the DVD, emphasizing the steps to facing fear. Write the steps on poster board to highlight graded exposure. Ask the following questions during the discussion: "How do you think the child felt at first? What was he thinking?"

2. *Generate a new problem:* Select a problem for the group to work on together. Feel free to use any one of the problems that were just identified in the parent–child group. If the children cannot agree on a problem situation, have a few problems prewritten on slips of paper so that one child can randomly select a problem situation to address. On a large poster board, draw a picture of a boy who looks stressed; include space around him to include what he is thinking and feeling with regard to the problematic situation. Draw a path from the stressed boy to another picture of a boy who appears calm. An example of this setup is included on the next page. Have the group generate strategies to "turn" the stressed boy into the calm boy. The group will take turns drawing from a deck of cards, which includes suggestions for handling anxiety in the categories of *facing fears, helpful thoughts,* and *calming and/or relaxing activities.* As a child selects a card, he or she is asked to identify the appropriate category of strategy; once the category is identified, it may be written on the poster board and the stressed boy may move one step closer to becoming calm. The deck of cards also will include "free choice" in the categories of *helpful thoughts* and *calming and/or relaxing activities.* When the free choice card is drawn, the group can work together to make a suggestion and add it to the list on the poster board. Leave a blank space under each category for the group to generate one strategy per category. Eventually the stressed boy will make it home; that is, he will "become" the calm boy.

    If time allows, work on another problem. You may even wish to consider role-playing if the children like this kind of activity. At the end of this activity, summarize what the group has reviewed so that they can share this information with the larger group.

END—BACK TO LARGE GROUP

Stressed to Calm

Problem: _____

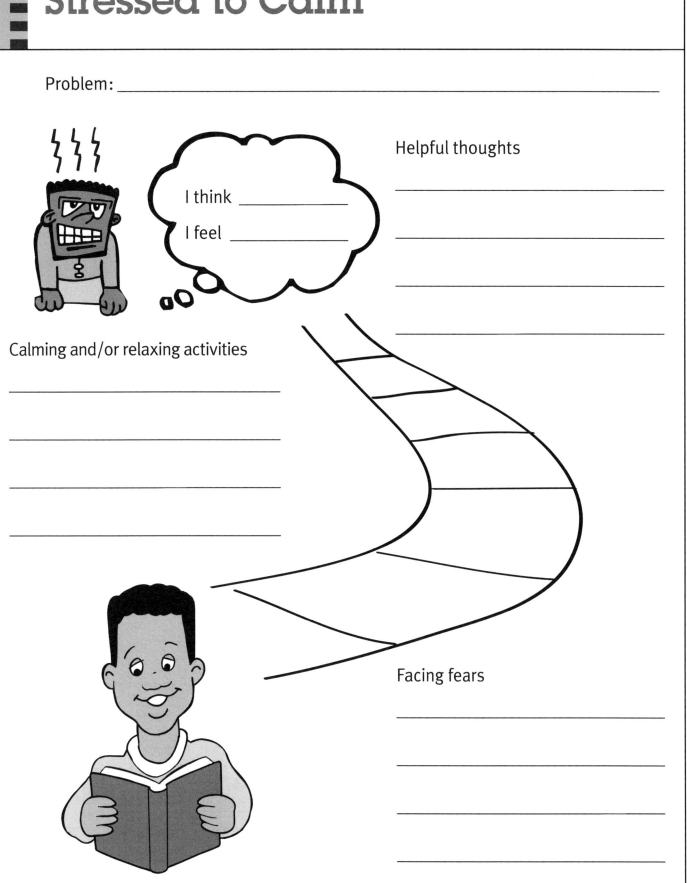

I think _____

I feel _____

Helpful thoughts

_____

_____

_____

_____

Calming and/or relaxing activities

_____

_____

_____

_____

Facing fears

_____

_____

_____

_____

▐▐▐▐▐▐ Large Group (Children and Parents Together)

Activity

1. *Closing/good-bye:*

   - *Share time:* The children can show their parents the stressed boy and how he changed to calm boy and made it "home." They can give examples of how they handled his fear and/or worry.
   - *Deep breathing.*

END BOOSTER

Session Notes

_____

_____

_____

_____

_____

_____

_____

_____

_____

_____

_____

_____

_____

_____

_____

_____

_____

_____

_____

References

American Psychiatric Association. (2000). *Diagnostic and statistical manual of mental disorder* (4th ed., text rev.). Washington, DC: Author.

Arnold, T. (1997). *Parts.* New York: Dial Books for Young Readers.

Arnold, T. (2001). *More Parts.* New York: Puffin Books.

Attwood, T. (2005). Cognitive behavioral therapy for children and adults with Asperger's syndrome. *Behavior Change, 21,* 147–161.

Barrett, P., Healy-Farrell, L., & March, J. (2004). Cognitive-behavioral family treatment of childhood obsessive-compulsive disorder. A controlled trial. *Journal of the Academy of Child and Adolescent Psychiatry, 43,* 46–62.

Bellini, S. (2004). Social skills deficits and anxiety in high-functioning adolescents with autism spectrum disorders. *Focus on Autism and Other Developmental Disabilities, 19*(2), 78–86.

Birmaher, B., Brent, D., Chiapetta, L., Bridge, J., Monga, S., & Baugher, M. (1999). Psychometric properties of the Screen for Child Anxiety Related Emotional Disorders (SCARED). *Journal of the American Academy of Child and Adolescent Psychiatry, 38,* 1230–1236.

Brereton, A.V., Tonge, B.J., & Einfeld, S.L. (2006). Psychopathology in children and adolescents with autism compared to young people with intellectual disability. *Journal of Autism and Developmental Disorders, 36,* 863–870.

Chalfant, A., Rapee, R., & Carroll, L. (2006). Treating anxiety disorders in children with high-functioning autism spectrum disorders: A controlled trial. *Journal of Autism and Developmental Disorders, 37,* 1842–57.

Chansky, T. (2004). *Freeing your child from anxiety.* New York: Broadway Books.

Cobham, V.E., Dadds, M.R., & Spence, S.H. (1998). The role of parental anxiety in the treatment of childhood anxiety. *Journal of Consulting and Clinical Psychology, 66,* 893–905.

Compton, S.N., March, J.S., Brent, D., Albano, A.M., Weersing, R., & Curry, J. (2004). Cognitive-behavioral psychotherapy for anxiety and depressive disorders in children and adolescents: An evidence-based medicine review. *Journal of American Academy of Child and Adolescent Psychiatry, 43,* 930–959.

Dadds, M.R., & Barrett, P.M. (2001). Practitioner review: Psychological management of anxiety disorders in childhood. *Journal of Child Psychology and Psychiatry, 42,* 999–1011.

Garland, E.J., & Clark, S.L. (1995). *Taming worry dragons: A manual for children, parents and other coaches.* Vancouver, Canada: British Columbia's Children's Hospital.

Gillott, A., Furniss, F., & Walter, A. (2001). Anxiety in high-functioning children with autism. *Autism, 5,* 277–286.

Greig, A., & MacKay, T. (2005). Asperger's syndrome and cognitive behaviour therapy: New applications for educational psychologists. *Educational and Child Psychology, 22,* 4–15.

Guy, W., & Bonato, R.R. (Eds). (1976). *CGI clinical global impressions. Manual for the EDCEU Assessment Battery* (Rev. ed., pp. 12-1–12-6). Chevy Chase, MD: National Institute of Mental Health.

Hare, D.J. (1997). The use of cognitive-behavioral therapy with people with Asperger syndrome: A case study. *Autism, 1,* 215–225.

Jahn-Clough, L. (1994). *Alicia has a bad day.* Boston: Houghton Mifflin.

Kendall, P., & Beidas, R. (2007). Smoothing the trail for dissemination of evidence-based practices for youth: Flexibility within fidelity. *Professional Psychology: Research and Practice, 38,* 13–20.

Kendall, P.C., Brady, E.U., & Verduin, T. (2001). Comorbidity in childhood anxiety disorders and treatment outcome. *Journal of the American Academy of Child and Adolescent Psychiatry, 40,* 787–794.

Kendall, P.C., & Hedtke, K. (2006). *Coping cat workbook* (2nd ed.). Ardmore, PA: Workbook Publishing.

Lainhart, J.E. (1999). Psychiatric problems in individuals with autism, their parents and siblings. *International Review of Psychiatry, 11,* 278–298.

Leyfer, O., Folstein, S., Bacalman, S., Davis, N., Dinh, E., Morgan, J., et al. (2006). Comorbid psychiatric disorders in children with autism: Interview development and rates of disorders. *Journal of Autism and Developmental Disorders, 36,* 849–861.

Lord, C. (1995). Treatment of a high-functioning adolescent with autism: A cognitive-behavioral approach. In M.A. Reinecke & F.M. Dattilio (Eds.), *Cognitive therapy with children and adolescents: A casebook for clinical practice* (pp. 394–404). New York: Guilford Press.

March, J., & Mulle, K. (1998). *OCD in children and adolescents: A cognitive-behavioral treatment manual.* New York: Guilford Press.

Mendlowitz, S., Manassis, K., Bradley S., Scapillato, D. Mjezitis, S., & Shaw, B. (1999). Cognitive-behavioral group treatments in childhood anxiety disorders: The role of parental involvement. *Journal of the American Academy of Child and Adolescent Psychiatry, 38,* 1233–1229.

Muris, P., Steerneman, P., Merckelbach, H., Holdrinet, I., & Meesters, C. (1998). Comorbid anxiety symptoms in children with pervasive developmental disorder. *Journal of Anxiety Disorders, 12,* 387–393.

National Autism Center. (2009). *National Standards Report.* Retrieved from http://www.nationalautismcenter.org/ pdf/NAC%20Standards%20Report.pdf

Rapee, R., Wignall, A., Hudson, J., & Schniering, C. (2000). *Treating anxious children and adolescents: An evidence based approach.* Oakland, CA: Harbinger Publications.

Reaven, J., Blakeley-Smith, A., Culhane-Shelburne, K., & Hepburn, S. (manuscript in preparation). *A randomized trial: group cognitive behavior therapy for children with high-functioning autism spectrum disorders and anxiety.*

Reaven, J., Blakeley-Smith, A., Nichols, S., Dasari, M., Flanigan, E., & Hepburn, S. (2009). Cognitive behavioral group treatment for anxiety symptoms in children with high-functioning autism spectrum disorders: A pilot study. *Focus on Autism and Other Developmental Disabilities, 24,* 27–37.

Reaven, J., & Hepburn, S. (2003). Cognitive-behavioral treatment of obsessive-compulsive disorder in a child with Asperger's syndrome: A case report. *Autism, 7,* 145–164.

Reaven, J., & Hepburn, S. (2006). The parent's role in the treatment of anxiety symptoms in children with high-functioning autism spectrum disorders. *Mental Health Aspects of Developmental Disabilities, 9,* 73–80.

Russell, E., & Sofronoff, K. (2005). Anxiety and social worries in children with Asperger syndrome. *Australian and New Zealand Journal of Psychiatry, 39,* 633–638.

Silverman, W., & Albano, A. (1996). *Anxiety disorders in-* *terview schedule for children for DSM-IV: (Child and parent versions).* San Antonio, TX: Psychological Corporation/Graywind.

Sofronoff, K., Attwood, T., & Hinton, S. (2005). A randomized controlled trial of a CBT intervention for anxiety in children with Asperger syndrome. *Journal of Child Psychology and Psychiatry, 46,* 1152–1160.

Sze, K.M., & Wood, J.J. (2007). Cognitive behavioral treatment of comorbid anxiety disorders and social difficulties in children with high-functioning autism: A case report. *Journal of Contemporary Psychotherapy 3,* 133–143.

Velting, O.N., Setzer, N.J., & Albano, A.M. (2004). Update on and advances in assessment and cognitive-behavioral treatment of anxiety disorders in children and adolescents. *Professional Psychology: Research and Practice, 35*(1), 42–54.

Viorst, J. (1972) *Alexander and the terrible, horrible, no good, very bad day.* New York: Aladdin Paperbacks.

Walkup, J., Albano, A., Piacentini, J., Birmaher, B., Compton, S., Sherrill, J., et al. (2008). Cognitive-behavioral therapy, sertraline, or a combination in childhood anxiety. *The New England Journal of Medicine, 359,* 2753–2766.

White, M., & Epston, D. (1990). *Narrative means to therapeutic ends.* New York: Norton.

White, S.W., Ollendick, T., Scahill, L., Oswald, D., Albano, A.M. (2009). Preliminary efficacy of a cognitive-behavioral treatment program for anxious youth with autism spectrum disorders. *Journal of Autism and Developmental Disorders, 39,* 1652–1662.

Wood, J., Drahota, A., Sze, K., Har, K., Chiu, A., & Langer, D. (2009). Cognitive behavioral therapy for anxiety in children with autism spectrum disorders: A randomized, controlled trial. *Journal of Child Psychiatry and Psychology, 50*(3), 224–234.

Index